STEADFAST Love

"*Steadfast Love* served to remind me that over and over again in His Word, God assures me that He loves with an overwhelming, everlasting, extravagant love . . . and it's for *me*! What amazing grace!"

Angela Elwell Hunt
Author of *The Tale of Three Trees*

STEADFAST Love

DEBBIE ALSDORF

Cook Communications

Faithful Woman is an imprint of
Cook Communications Ministries, Colorado Springs, Colorado 80918
Cook Communications, Paris, Ontario
Kingsway Communications, Eastbourne, England

Printed in the United States of America

1 2 3 4 5 6 7 8 9 10 Printing/Year 04 03 02 01 00

Unless otherwise noted, all Scripture references are taken from the *Holy Bible, New International Version* ®. Copyright © 1973, 1978, 1984 by International Bible Society. Used by permission of Zondervan Publishing House. All rights reserved. Additional Scripture taken from *The Amplified Bible Old Testament* (AMP), © 1962, 1964 by Zondervan Publishing House; *The Amplified Bible New Testament* (AMP), © 1954, 1958 The Lockman Foundation; *The Message* (TM) copyright © 1993. Used by permission of NavPress Publishing House; *King James Version* (KJV).

Editor: Afton Rorvik
Cover Design: David Thomason
Interior Design: Lisa A. Barnes

Library of Congress Cataloging-in-Publication Data

Alsdorf, Debbie.
    Steadfast love / by Debbie Alsdorf.
        p.cm.
    ISBN 0-7814-3384-3
    1. God—Love—Biblical teaching. 2. Bible—Study and teaching. 3. Christian women—Religious life. I. Title.

BS544 .A47 2000
241'.4—dc21   00-027263

Dedicated to
the women of Cornerstone Fellowship:
May you continue to grow in the knowledge of God's love for you.

&

In memory of my mother
Irene Kenzie
who now rests in the arms of God's love.

*"And so we know and rely
on the love God has for us."*
1 John 4:16

ACKNOWLEDGMENTS

Many people have given me consistent encouragement and support. They have prayed and trusted God to get the message of His unchanging love into more hands and more hearts. God has used their encouragement to get this material into print. I would like to thank the following for expressing God's love to me:

Pastor Steve Madsen and Brenda Madsen for all the encouragement, trust, and freedom you give me to serve with my heart's passion the women at Cornerstone Fellowship.

The pastoral staff at Cornerstone for being the most awesome team of men and women with whom anyone could hope to serve.

Betty Ellis for insisting that this material should be published and praying me through all the steps.

Teri Collins for sending the materials through the prison system and for encouraging me to spread the news of God's love.

Special editors who helped shape this study . . . Julie Smith and Afton Rorvik, thank you for making this experience a joy. Julie, thanks for believing in me and paving the way for a first-time author.

My friends who cheered me on . . . Patti Esser, Donna Burke, Lisa Woodworth, Julie Fox, Liz Grundvig, Diane Linse, Norine Thornock, Eileen Terpstra, Lavon Ribera, Triona McCracken.

My sister Sharon, a sister and friend of the heart.

My husband Ray, and the wonderful kids we are blessed to love: Justin and Cameron Brier, Ashley and Megan Alsdorf.

And . . . most especially the Lord Jesus Christ who continues to fill me with the truth that His love for me is *Steadfast . . . fixed, firm, and unchanging.*

CONTENTS

*I*NTRODUCTION

Most of us know the song "Jesus Loves Me." But, do we know the powerful truth behind the words of that classic? It is a truth that is life-changing. A truth that can heal our hearts and bring answers to individual areas of insecurity and fear. When you understand the love of God for you personally, your life will change dramatically.

Where do you go to find out the truth of God's love? You spend time in the pages of His love letters just for you—*the Bible*.

If you've been looking for confidence, personal worth, and healthy self-esteem then you need to soak in His love for you. Everything starts and ends with understanding God's love. It is basic . . . yet powerful!

As a Christian, I overlooked the love of God for many years. I thought I understood God's love. Then I began to realize that if I really believed in His love, I would not be so afraid, anxious, and insecure. When the pieces of my life fell apart, I realized that the only thing that could put me back together again was to go deeper with God. It was in understanding the love of Jesus for me personally that I found the deep, rich walk with Him that I always wanted. I went back to the basics and started clinging to them for life, and it was there that I found all I will ever need. For it was in this place that I found the *steadfast love of God for me*, which is fixed, firm, and unchanging.

This study is more than just a book in which to neatly pen your answers. If you just look up the answers, dutifully putting in your time, you will not digest all that this spiritual food was meant to accomplish in your heart and minds. But, if you take time to savor the words you will read in your Bible, lingering over them, enjoying them, and really tasting them, you will be experiencing what the Bible refers to as, "meditating on the Word of God" (Psalm 119). The references you will be looking up are living and active (Hebrews 4:12), meant to be life-giving soul food, offering instruction and direction for daily living (2 Timothy 3:16). When you meditate on God's Word instead of just speed reading it, you will have an interaction with your maker and your personal relationship with Him will come alive.

This is meant to be an **Interactive Bible Study.** In order for this to be accomplished, you must interact with the Word of God on a personal level. This study is not for the purpose of giving you more head knowledge. Instead, as the truth goes from head to heart, my hope is that this study will change your life.

The Bible is to be the manual by which we live. Manuals are practical and informative. The Bible is indeed practical as well as informative and personal. We wouldn't think of trying to operate a sewing machine with the instructions from a washing machine manual. But, for some reason we keep trying to operate our lives with instructions other than the Word of God, which is our maker's manual for each of us.

This study concentrates on two very important facts: 1) you were made **by God** and 2) you were made **for God** (Colossians 1:16); You will know an unspeakable, unshakable peace that fills you completely when you learn to rest in the God of love, who made you and has plans just for you. You will discover that you are a limited edition, God's treasure. No one on earth is exactly you. Discover who you are in God's love and begin to live with purpose and passion.

Be sure to personalize this study all the way through. It is your journey, your experience with God, and the revelation of His love for you. I also encourage you to pray before you do each lesson. Before you begin to study each time, ask the Holy Spirit to teach you and show you the truth in God's Word. Through His Spirit, God will make His Word real and applicable to you today.

You can do this study individually, with a friend, or in a group. If you do it individually, you may want to take your time, working through the book at God's prompting. You should plan to do some of the study each day, savoring each truth, thinking about how it relates to you and praying for understanding.

If you do this study in a group, I suggest you work through one chapter a week. Each chapter has twelve to fifteen sections. These can easily be divided into a five-day block, by doing three sections each day.

The most important thing is that you take your time and don't rush. Set some time aside, even if it is just ten to fifteen minutes to do nothing but soak in Scripture. You will need a Bible, a dictionary, and a thesaurus. It would also be helpful for you to purchase a blank book in which you can write some personal thoughts as you work through the lessons.

Though this is a basic study, don't be fooled into thinking there isn't enough in it for you. These foundational truths of God's Word are deep and powerful. I am daily learning more of the reality of God's love for me. This reality is changing my life. I am praying that His love will make a dramatic difference in your life too!

Wanting God's best for you,

Debbie Alsdorf

TIPS FOR GROUP MEMBERS

When working through this study in a group, the following suggestions may prove helpful.

- Have a purpose for your time together. What do you hope to accomplish in twelve weeks?

- Keep in step with the lesson, giving opportunity for personal sharing on the topic of each lesson and the message of each Scripture passage.

- Encourage one another to be real and provide a safe place for that.

- Keep all group conversation and sharing Christ-centered and confidential.

- Encourage practical application of each week's lesson, holding each other accountable.

- Pray before you begin, and pray when you end.

TIPS FOR GROUP LEADERS

It is a privilege to lead other women into an understanding of God's love. The following suggestions may help you lead each woman in your group in her personal journey.

- Make every effort to stay on track so that you study the Bible rather than just functioning as a social or support group. Though both social interaction and support are important, the main emphasis should first be the personal application and study of God's Word. (As you know, women can get off track!)

- Promote fellowship and unity within the group by accepting each woman right where she is today. Have a "No Stones" policy—women agree not to judge or throw stones at another woman who is struggling and seeking understanding within the group.

- Nurture each woman in her spiritual gifts, personal holiness, and in her interaction with the Word of God.

- Be real so that others have the freedom to be real too.

- Be honest as you work through the study so that others can feel safe confessing their faults and find healing as they learn to apply God's Word.

- Provide a place that is safe, loving, and nurturing.

- Pray for each woman in your group and take seriously the privilege of leading her in a study of God's Word.

THE RELATIONSHIP OF LOVE

"Love the Lord your God with all your heart and with all your soul and with all your mind"
(Matt. 22:37).

Being a Christian is not about doing all the right things, following a set of rules, or adhering to certain rituals. Being a Christian is a matter of the heart. It is all about a relationship with the God of the Universe and the creator of all things.

Religion is a belief in a supernatural power and an adherence to a set of rules and regulations. Relationship is the connection with that power. While religion is the head knowledge of spiritual things, relationship is the heart, connecting with the things of the spirit. It is possible to be religious while not having any personal relationship with God. This kind of religious experience is empty and frustrating.

Many people grow up in homes that teach religion in some form or another. I did. I grew up in a home where Sunday church attendance was an absolute priority, but we never talked about God in our home except during a small handful of emergencies. Then we would say our memorized prayers and cry our eyes out to God for help. But, once the crisis was over and we were back to the daily business of living, God was out of sight and out of mind. He seemed far away, perched up on a cloud somewhere watching to see if I was being a good little girl.

Because my family went to church, I guess I had religion. I know I didn't have a relationship with God. I had no idea what it meant to connect with God or what it meant to have my life tied into Him and His plans. My life was all about my plans and my dreams. I had no idea that God had plans for my life and that finding purpose in Him would be more fulfilling than all my own dreams.

To many of us God sometimes seems so far away and removed from real life. But, actually, I've come to learn that He is quite interested and involved with every one of us each day. I now know that He has given us access to a personal relationship with Himself through His Son Jesus Christ. 1 Timothy 2:5-6 tells us, "For there is one God and one mediator between God and men, the man Christ Jesus, who gave himself as a ransom for all men."

Do you have a personal relationship with God through His Son Jesus? This may sound like a basic question, but it is an important one. This is not a trick question. You obviously know with whom you have relationships. Don't misunderstand the question. I am not asking, "Do you go to church?" I am asking you, "Do you know Jesus? Do you know who He was, why He came, what He taught, and who He is today?" This is a question of relationship with God, and it is a personal question.

Perhaps you have been a Christian for many years, but still deep inside you are frustrated, hurting, insecure, and anxious much of the time. You keep thinking that your belief in God should be making a difference in your life. Let me ask you a question: Do you have *a love relationship with God?* I am not referring to the decision that leads to salvation, or the completion of religious achievements or rituals. Rather, I am asking if you have the daily connecting with God that makes him Lord and master of your life.

Come, let us return to the Lord. . . . he will heal us . . . he will bind up our wounds. . . . he will revive us . . . he will restore us, that we may live in his presence (Hosea 6:1–2).

There is a big difference between knowing about God in your head and experiencing God in the very depths of your ordinary, everyday existence. Experiencing God requires relationship. It requires a love relationship of the heart. Perhaps it has been a long time since you have been that up close and personal with Him. Or, perhaps you have never known that you could be. It is in this close personal relationship with God that we experience healing, restoration, and the ultimate peace for which we all long.

1. What do you think it means to have a relationship with God?

∽ Read Hosea 6:1-2. According to this verse, when we return to God what does He do? (Keep in mind that *revive* means to bring back to life and strength. *Restore* means to bring back to an original state by repairing or rebuilding.)

Our original state was "naked and unashamed."[1] Today when we are in relationship with God, we have the freedom to be real with ourselves and real with others, unashamed of our weaknesses, embracing His healing and strength. But, we have all been wounded in real life and have at times traveled far from that original state of close personal fellowship with God. When away from God we become afraid[2] and try desperately to cover ourselves. We hide behind masks while covering up the beauty God created in us. When we come back into relationship with Him, He heals our wounds and brings us back to spiritual life again. Returning is something we should do each day when we wake up—returning again to the Lord, day by day.

> *What is a relationship? It is an association between two or more things; a connection, interdependence, link; a tie in, hook up.*[3]

> Have you ever pondered the significance of the simple phrase, "God loves you?" It may embody the most important truth anyone can grasp: that God has called us into a loving relationship with Himself. Our part is simply to trust and believe in the deep care and compassion God freely extends to us. How beautiful it is to experience the freedom and joy of a love relationship with God! [4] —*Chuck Smith*

∽ When you return to God, He enables you to live in His presence. Look up *presence* in the dictionary and write out the definition.

∽ How does the definition help you understand the meaning of living in the *presence* of God?

2. **Have you ever thought about what living in the presence of God would mean to you personally? What would change?**

Living in the presence of God is living in the state of believing He is always present with us, actively at work and alive in us. It is living with the constant remembrance of Jesus who lived to please the Father. It is living to do those things we know God loves because we love Him and have a relationship with Him. It is not living by a set of rules but rather by the code of a heart in tune with its maker.

∽ Read Hosea 6:3. Write out the key words.

Yes, let us know—recognize, be acquainted with, and understand Him: let us be zealous to know the Lord—to appreciate, give heed to and cherish Him (Hosea 6:3, AMP).

∽ How do you acknowledge the Lord in your life?

This Bible study is about knowing God. It is about being acquainted with Him. It is about going from a "crisis relationship" with Christ to an "everyday relationship." Many of us are not connected to Him, even after years of being a Christian. Some of us are connected to programs, ministries, theologies, and good works, but we are still not connected to God. Sadly, many of us do not understand His love and therefore we serve out of obligation, fear, or a desire to please people, rather than serving out of a love relationship with our maker.

The Priority of Relationship

Activity, though essential to practical faith, is not a substitute for personal fellowship. It can never outweigh intimacy with God. Our relationship with Christ erodes and cools when our primary focus is taken off the Messiah and placed on other things. That is the beginning of idolatry, and it is a dangerous path for the saint to tread. The gods of this age—sports, work, money—are cleverly disguised and ensnare many Christians with their compelling allegiance. Too much of a good thing can be wrong if it distracts you from devotion to Christ.[5] —*Charles Stanley*

3. **First love (priority love) gives God first place. On a scale of 1-10, what place does a relationship with God rank in your life? Why?**

∞ How would you describe your present relationship with God?

∞ Write out Psalm 139:3.

∞ Write out Psalm 139:23-24.

In Psalm 139:3 we see clearly that God had a relationship with David. God was familiar with all of David's ways. In the same way God is familiar with us. In verses 23-24 we read more about David's relationship with God. He is asking God to search him and to know him. David trusted God to search the deepest part of him, exposing anything that would be unhealthy to his spiritual growth. Like David, we also can have this sort of relationship with

God. It is a personal interaction that is not dependent on another's actions, approval, or faith. It is our own personal interaction and experience with God.

⚭ What does a love relationship with God mean to you?

> ... that is the greatest joy in life—to experience a genuine love relationship with God. To know that He is for us, that He loves us, is the greatest source of security any person will ever know. Discovering the glorious grace of God was one of the most important events in my whole spiritual experience. I learned to relate to God on an entirely new basis: not on the basis of my works, or of my righteousness, but on the basis of God's love for me through Jesus Christ.[6]—*Chuck Smith*

---

4. **Read 1 Corinthians chapter 13. After reading chapter 13, go back up to the last verse of chapter 12 and note that it says: "And now I will show you the most excellent way." What do you think the Apostle Paul meant by that statement?**

⚭ Read 1 Corinthians 13:2-3. What do you gain by good works or spiritual gifts alone?

In 1 Corinthians 13:2 we see Paul expressing that even if he had all knowledge and great faith he would be nothing without the Love of God. How often we search for things that will make us seem more knowledgeable, more spiritual, and more enviable. Even as Christians we turn to people and things much more readily than we turn to God. Often we bypass God's love as if it were some fluffy extra that we don't need. We get down to the real work of serving and doing things for God. In reality He is most interested in who we are on the inside. What I do for God is not nearly as important as who I am with God. There is a big difference. Embracing His love is the most excellent way.

Defining God's Love

∽ Make a list of the characteristics of God's love toward you as outlined in 1 Corinthians chapter 13:4-7.

GOD'S LOVE IS:	HOW GOD SHOWS HIS LOVE TO ME:
Patient	He is always patient with me when I _____.

Often we only look at the Love Chapter (1 Corinthians 13) as a list of ways we are to behave, and we use it to generate a set of rules. We conclude that we are to be more patient, kind, etc. Right now I encourage you to look at this chapter as the characteristics of *God's love toward you.* Don't look at who you need to be, look at who God is. This is personal.

You may feel as if you have blown it big time, and that there is no hope. But then you read 1 Corinthians 13:5: "God keeps no record of wrongs." I hope you will begin to be filled with hope and absolute adoration for this God who is so tender, loving, and forgiving.

∞ What characteristic of God's love means the most to you today? Explain.

5. **What does love NEVER do? (See 1 Corinthians 13:8.)**

∞ Write out Lamentations 3:21-23.

∞ What is "new every morning" for you?

∞ Can you apply this personally to your life today? In what specific area do you need God's great love, faithfulness, and compassion?

6. **Read 1 Chronicles 28:20. David had given his son Solomon a task. What was Solomon's attitude to be toward what now lay ahead of him?**

∞ Why could he have this attitude?

∞ What was the promise?

∞ What did God promise not to do in any circumstance?

Now back up to 1 Chronicles 28:9-10. This chapter in the Old Testament records David's plans for the temple and David's instruction to his son Solomon, regarding the temple. God was calling Solomon to build something important—a sanctuary. In order for Solomon to complete the work, he had to be strong. We see in verse 9 the following keys to the type of love relationship with God that would produce strength for anything and everything Solomon was called to do. These keys will also give us the strength for all that God has planned for us as individuals.

7. **Journal your thoughts on each of the following key sentences, taken from 1 Chronicles 28:9-10.**

   • Acknowledge God.

   • Serve Him with your whole heart.

   • Serve Him with devotion.

   • Serve Him with a willing mind.

   • Seek Him.

When you are in a relationship with God, you will become strong and secure because you will realize that He is with you and will never fail you. His love is new every morning, and that is enough to give all of us courage and joy! But . . . how do we get all this wonderful stuff from our heads to our hearts and then into our everyday lives?

Here are our instructions:

"If you *seek Him,* He will be found by you" (1 Chronicles 28:9, italics added).

"He will restore us that we may *live in His presence*" (Hosea 6:2, italics added).

8. Write out James 1:5.

∽ Write out Matthew 7:7.

We must ask God to make His Word real to us and applicable to our lives. When we knock in prayer, we can be sure the door will open! This is a relationship of communicating with the Father. This is a relationship built by relying on Him, asking Him for wisdom, seeking His will, and knocking in prayer.

9. Read 1 Corinthians 2:11-16. What do these verses say to you about transferring God's truth from your head to your heart?

- According to these verses, who can make the truth of God's love real to you?

- According to the last verse, what do you have?

10. Read John 14:15-18. Who is with you forever?

∞ Read John 15:26. What does the Spirit do?

∞ Read John 16:5-14. How does the Spirit bring glory to Jesus?

∞ According to the previous three passages, what is the work of the Holy Spirit?

∞ How does the Holy Spirit work specifically in your life?

∞ Look up counselor, helper, and comforter in the dictionary and write down the definitions.
counselor:

helper:

comforter:

Have you ever prayed and asked God to pour out the power of the Holy Spirit on you, to guide you into the truth of God's love just for you?

Asking for the wisdom of the Holy Spirit to make God's love real and personal to you must be a starting point if you are going to experience the love of God in your daily life. I am excited to know that God has provided a helper, teacher, and counselor for me in the Holy Spirit. While the world is busy connecting to philosophies, I know that I can connect with the Spirit of the Living God.

All this is made possible by receiving Him: "Yet to all who received him, to those who believed in his name, he gave the right to become children of God—children born not of natural descent, nor of human decision or a husband's will, but born of God" (John 1:12-13).

I am His child, and He wants to teach me things about life, about love, and about Himself. While others are still searching for something to guide them, I can be assured that I have the best and most accurate guide around—the Spirit of God!

The Holy Spirit can and will make God's love real to you. Pray the Word of God, as written in John 16:13: ". . . he will guide you into all truth."

Father,

I ask you to lead me into an understanding of Your love for me and guide me into all truth regarding my value and purpose in Your plan. I ask you to do this by the power of your Spirit. Amen.

In a world that sends mixed messages about love, God can give us the right message regarding the love of God for us as individuals.

11. Write out 1 Corinthians 2:12.

∽ Do you believe God's love is something that has been freely given to you? Why or why not?

∽ How can the Holy Spirit give you fresh perspective and insight in this area?

12. Read Philippians 1:9. Copy this part of Paul's prayer.

∽ What did Paul say you needed regarding love?

It is clear that we can not understand the love of God and enter into a relationship with that love on our own. We need the Spirit of God to teach us and give us depth of insight.

There are many markers to success and value in our world. We need to understand God's marker of value and success if we are going to truly succeed. A relationship with God is God's marker of success. Psalm 1 says in part, "Blessed is the [woman] who delights in the Lord. . . . Whatever [she] does will prosper." (That is a successful woman!) We must pray to become lovers of God, rather than lovers of men.

13. Read John 5:39-40. What are your thoughts regarding this passage?

∞ Do you think you have refused to come to God for "life"?

You can have biblical knowledge coming out of your ears, but if you haven't come to God and connected with Him, you still need to *Get a Life!*

In the early church it was a definite characteristic of spiritual deficiency that the people lived to please other people rather than to please God. That is why He says they didn't have the love of God in their hearts (John 5:42). The religious people of that time had plenty of rules and regulations that governed their relationship with God. These rules all came tumbling down when Jesus reduced everything to one command: Love God with all your heart, soul, strength, and mind.

Many of you may have been turned off by rules in the church. Maybe Christ represents only rules to you. Well, Jesus Christ wants to represent love and life. This life is not about following man-made rules, but about following God.

14. Write out Matthew 22:37-38.

∽ Write out Deuteronomy 6:4-5.

In closing, I encourage you this week to concentrate on what it means to have a relationship with God. What does it mean to love Him with all of your being? Maybe this concept is new to you, or maybe God is using this study to take your current relationship with Him to new levels of commitment and surrender. Wherever you are in your relationship to God, be sure to ask God to keep you from things that would hinder your love and devotion to Him. Ask Him daily to fill you with the desire to love Him with all that is within you.

A spiritual journey isn't about "arriving" or finally "getting it together." We never arrive . . . that's heaven! But, we can always be growing. Growth is active— alive with hope and promise. Each new day we can be slowly and steadily deepening our connection to God.

In every circumstance remember that God is with you. With each step, remember He is alongside you. He is not far off and unable to hear you or see you. He is closer to you than you realize. His presence is real. All He claims to be is real.

> It is the most profound common sense of all to put our poor, weak, foolish and helpless selves into the care and keeping of the God who made us, who loves us, and who alone can care for us. When we yield to God, it means we then belong to God, and that we now have all His infinite power and infinite love at work on our side! What I am inviting you to do is this: yield yourself to Him. Take advantage of this amazing privilege that human words cannot even express . . . regardless of circumstances or consequences . . . yield.[7] —*Hannah Whitall Smith*

Let's remember to make the connection with God, inviting Him into our most personal thoughts and dreams. Ask His direction for living and read the Bible as if the pages were the blueprints for our life's design.

> There is a difference between memorizing Scripture and thinking biblically. There's a difference between knowing the words and experiencing their meaning. There is a difference between having sentences embedded in your head and having their impact embedded in your heart. There is a difference between "doing Christianity" and being a Christian. You can memorize all of the words, but if you've forgotten the music you still won't be able to sing the song.[8] —*Tim Hansel*

"May the words of my mouth and the meditation of my heart, be pleasing in your sight, O Lord, my Rock and my Redeemer" (Psalm 19:14).

Dear Lord,

May I be Your woman, from the inside out. May I never forget the music of Your love for me. Keep me from just doing things that have the look of spirituality. Instead, give me the gift of experiencing Your Spirit on a daily basis. Thank You for Your love. Thank You that I am Your child. Thank You for Your faithfulness and Your love that is new every morning. Amen.

GOD IS LOVE

"God is love. Whoever lives in love lives in God, and God in Him"(1 John 4:16).

In 1 John 4:16 we read that "God is love." It doesn't say that He loves, although we know that God does love us with unconditional love. This Scripture says that God *is* love. This is His nature, who He is. He will never be anything other than love because to be so would be contrary to His own nature.

Love is such a loose term these days that we often don't know what it really means anymore. It can refer to anything from a vague impression to the most sincere depth of emotion and commitment. We live in a time with a confused concept of love. We have grown up with fairy-tale love and false expectations and dreams. We have picked up the mixed messages of love.

That is exactly why it is so important to have our minds renewed by God's Word. We need to be asking ourselves, "What does the Bible say about love?"

We love many things. I love my family, shopping, having fun with friends, my cats, Pugs and Bailey, my darling little dog, Bubba . . . and of course chocolate. (Doesn't every woman love chocolate?!) Love's range is widespread. That is one of the reasons why it's hard for us to believe the depth of God's character when we read that He is love, and that He loves us. We often reduce His love to a generality instead of embracing it as the life affirming truth that it is.

In this lesson we will begin looking closely at God's love, and His nature of love. We will examine it and think about how it affects us in a personal and practical way. I encourage you to focus only on your relationship to that love. This lesson's focus is not on you loving others, or any performance relating to love. Instead, this lesson encourages you to breathe in a deep fresh breath of God's love *just for you*. Let this lesson be personal! Let it be a building block in your relationship with God. Your trust in God's love nature is critical. It is my prayer that as you do this lesson, you will come to understand more fully that God is Love, and that He always works in and through your life with that love.

1. **Read Psalm 117. Now, write it out in the space provided.**

∽ Psalm 117 has only two verses. But, those two verses contain a powerful message. What are the two things that this psalm says about God's relationship toward you? Personalize this!

∽ What does this psalm tell you to do?

(Note: *extol* means to praise God highly. How do we do that? Well, in real everyday terms that would mean: thanking Him, honoring Him, worshiping Him, speaking and singing to Him—declaring His goodness!)

2. **Is the message of His enduring love encouraging to you? If not, why not?**

The message of God's love is hard for some people to grasp. Life is not always easy, and we are often disappointed with the way things turned out in our lives. Sometimes we blame our circumstances, sometimes we blame others, and often we blame ourselves. There are even times when we blame God. Some blame God openly, and others silently hide their disappointment. How many times the Lord must have heard,

"If You really are a God of love, why did You let this happen?" or, " *You are God! You could have prevented this!"*

Never allow yourself to question His love. Settle the truth of God's love in your heart and mind. He created you for a love relationship, one in which He always acts in love toward you. For Him to act otherwise would be a contradiction of who He is. He deals with our lives in a personal, loving fashion. We must respond with a personal interaction and relationship. No one can interact with the Lord for you. It's your relationship.

> Certain things no one can do for you. . . . You don't say, "I'm in love with that wonderful person, but romance is such a hassle. I'm going to hire a surrogate lover to enjoy the romance in my place. I'll hear about it and be spared the inconvenience." Who would do that? Perish the thought. You want the romance firsthand. You don't want to miss a word or a date, and you certainly don't want to miss the kiss, right? Certain things no one can do for you.[1]—*Max Lucado*

Every dealing God has had with you is an expression of love. If you really believe that God's nature is love, you will accept that His will and way in your life is love. Even when things happen that you don't understand, you can be assured that He has not left you even for a moment. His love is with you even in the darkest tunnel, the most frightening storm, and in the stillness of loneliness.

His will and way in your life is always best. He isn't a God of second best when we walk in His ways. If you have trouble settling this in your heart, you need to ask God to show you what is keeping you from believing wholeheartedly in His love.

So many of us have "worn out faith." Our faith has become worn out from the hardships and disappointments of life. We struggle to believe that God is the loving father the Bible says He is. This can happen when we expect God to be some Fairy God-Father in the sky, supplying all our dreams and wishes. Often we are so focused on what we want out of life— our plans, circumstances going our way, our goals and dreams, other people and their approval, or things—that we neglect to focus on knowing God, and forget to pray that His will be done in our lives. When things go wrong, we fall apart and run from the love that God has for us. We become disappointed, depleted, and worn out.

Have you been blaming yourself, others, or God? Perhaps it is time to ask Him to teach you about His love for you and His way of looking at life.

2. Read Psalm 17:6-7. What adjectives are used to describe God's love?

> *I have called upon You, O God, for You will hear me; incline Your ear to me and hear my speech. Show Your marvelous loving-kindness, O You Who save by Your right hand those who trust and take refuge in You from those who rise up against them (Psalm 17:6–7, AMP).*

Do you want to KNOW the wonder of His great love?

∞ Look up *wonder* in the dictionary. Write the definition here.

∞ Look up *great* in the dictionary and write the definition.

It is a remarkable thing that God loves us. We are imperfect. We fail and are often rebellious and weak. But God's love does not depend on our goodness at all. In fact, thinking we are "good" can be a trap that keeps us from further understanding God's love. Because God's love is not based on our performance, His love is an excellent thing . . . a surprise . . . a marvel. It is a wonder!

His love is great! I love this definition of great: "much above average, in size, amount, or intensity." Another definition of great is: "important." Using those definitions, we can then read Psalm 17:7 this way: "Show the wonder of your *important* love." Or we can read it: "Show the wonder of your love that is above all average loves . . . more intense, bigger than any other and more important than any love I have ever known or will ever know."

∞ Do you think it is important to understand God's love for you individually? Why or why not?

4. Read Ephesians 3:16-19. This is Paul's prayer for the church in Ephesus. What does verse 16 say Paul desired for the Ephesians?

∞ What power can strengthen you in your inner being?

5. Write out Psalm 109:21-22.

Stop right now and call on God as David did in the psalm above. Communicate to Him about your hurts and needs. Have you been disappointed, or are you stuck in a rut of worn out faith? Tell God about your heart, its condition, and its need for His love.

6. Write out Ephesians 3:16.

Stop right now and pray this for yourself. Ask the Lord, out of His glorious riches, to strengthen you with power through His Spirit in your inner being.

> The scripture plainly teaches that the gift of the Holy Spirit is a universal gift to all believers. . . .We must believe, therefore, that this unspeakable gift, which is meant to help us enter into the glorious realms of the Spirit now, is already the possession of even the weakest and most failing child of God. It is true,

whether we recognize His presence or not, whether we acknowledge and obey His control or not. He is within each of us. . . .The secret is that we must allow Him to take full possession. We are His sanctuary, His dwelling place, although we may not yet have opened every inward chamber of our hearts to let Him dwell therein . . . simply recognize the presence of God already within you, and fully submit to His ownership, and allow Him to control every circumstance.[21] —*Hannah Whitall Smith*

The Message paraphrases Ephesians 3:16-19 this way:

I ask him to strengthen you by his Spirit—not a brute strength but a glorious inner strength—that Christ will live in you as you open the door and invite him in. And I ask him that with both feet planted firmly on love, you'll be able to take in with all Christians the extravagant dimensions of Christ's love. Reach out and experience the breadth! Test its length! Plumb the depths! Rise to the heights! Live full lives, full in the fullness of God. God can do anything, you know—far more than you could ever imagine or guess or request in your wildest dreams! He does it, not by pushing us around, but by working within us, his Spirit deeply and gently within us."

∽ What do these verses say to you? (Take your time, and think about these verses. Read them over a few times out loud. Journal your thoughts.

(Note: If you have never written in a spiritual journal, this would be a wonderful time to begin. Often when we write out our feelings and prayers, it helps us to define where we are and what God is speaking to us personally.

You may want to get a book to journal in. It can be a pretty book that is sold at a stationary store or it can be a simple, spiral binder. You should keep your book handy to write in each time you sit down to read the Bible. Then you can jot down verses and what they mean to you. You can also record what God is speaking to your heart that day. There is no right or wrong in what you might write. So, fill your blank pages with prayers, Scripture, poems, wishes, and dreams—or whatever God is quietly speaking just to you.)

7. Write out 1 John 3:16. How would you describe this kind of love?

8. Write out and reflect on Romans 5:8. (Make notes on your thoughts.)

∞ Write out and reflect on 1 John 4:9-10.

9. Write out and reflect on 1 John 4:15–16. On what does this verse say you should know and rely?

∞ According to 1 John 4:15-16, what describes God?

10. Write out John 15:9. (These are the words of Christ . . . love those red letters!)

∽ According to John 15:9, where are you to remain?

If we are to remain "in" something, we must pray to understand what that means. According to the dictionary, *remain* means: to continue without change; to stay after the removal or loss of others; to be left as still to be dealt with; to endure/persist.

Throughout this study I will be referring to three *R's*:

Remain in God. How do we remain in His love? (Read John 15:10-11.) This is a key to living each day in a personal relationship with the Father.

Renew yourself in Him daily. Romans 12:2 says "be transformed by the renewing of your mind." Our minds should be renewed with the words of truth found within the pages of the Bible.

Rest. Philippians 4:6-7 tells us: "Do not be anxious about anything, but in everything, by prayer and petition with thanksgiving, present your requests to God. And the peace of God, which transcends all understanding, will guard your hearts and your minds in Christ Jesus." Peace is rest!

Whenever I am out of sorts, I like to use the *R's* as a check system.

Am I **remaining** today? Am I connected, abiding in Christ?

Am I **renewed** today? Have I read or meditated or thought about His Word?

Am I **resting** today? Have I prayed and turned my life over to God?

Usually one of the *R's* will be missing, sometimes all of them. Then I need to go back to God and reconnect with Him. That is what it is all about—a connection with God.

We read the Word, we pray. We connect, and we rest in Jesus. We will never understand the love of God unless we get to know Him through His Word and through a personal relationship with Him.

11. Write out John 3:16.

∽ Now personalize this verse in your heart by writing it with your own name.

For God so loved _____

12. Write Romans 5:8 in your own words.

The sacrificial love of Jesus Christ is a type of love that is foreign to us. It's hard for us to comprehend unconditional love because we live in a world of conditions. It's hard for us to love those who don't love us, disappoint us, hurt us, or ultimately fail us. But, Christ in His goodness has the Ultimate Love, in that while we were plain "yuk" He died for us. And the best news is that this same love protects and establishes us all the days of our lives. Isaiah 45:22 says, "Turn to Me, and be saved. . . ." Don't mull around in your "stuff," trying to figure out how God could possibly save you, just look to Him.

> Many of us have a mental picture of what a Christian should be, and looking at this image in other Christian's lives becomes a hindrance to our focusing on God. This is not salvation—it is not simple enough. He says, in effect, "Look to Me and you are saved," not "You will be saved someday." We will find what we are looking for if we will concentrate on Him. We get distracted from God and irritable with Him while He continues to say to us, 'Look to Me, and be saved. . . ." Our difficulties, our trials, and our worries about tomorrow all vanish when we look to God. Wake yourself up and look to God. Build your hope on Him. No matter how many things seem to be pressing in on you, be determined to push them aside and look to him. "Look to Me. . . ." Salvation is yours the moment you look.[3]—*Oswald Chambers*

Do you realize that His Spirit is working deeply and gently within you today? It is His desire that we *know* His love, and it is His desire that we look to Him each day. The love of Jesus Christ must be the foundation of our lives. It is in knowing this love that we have peace and fullness and are able to be vessels through which God's love can ultimately be poured out to others, bringing them into the knowledge of Jesus Christ.

13. Pick the verse that spoke to you the most from this lesson. Write it here and then memorize it this week. You may also want to write it on an index card and carry it with you as a reminder.

> *This love holds nothing back, but, in a manner which no human mind can fathom, makes thee one with itself. Oh wondrous love, to love us even as the Father loved Him, and to offer us this love as our every-day dwelling!"* — *Andrew Murray*

Tell yourself the following truth this week:
God's love is fixed, firm, unchanging.
His love is a REALITY in my life.

I love You fervently and devotedly, O Lord, my strength. The Lord is my rock, my fortress, and my deliverer: my God, my keen and firm strength in Whom I will trust and take refuge, my shield, and the horn of my salvation, my high tower (Psalm 18:1–2, AMP).

Dear Lord,

May I know the love of God in a way unlike I have ever known it before. I desire to remain in that same love that first loved me and sought me out while I was turned the other way. By the power of Your Spirit, may I remain in You, renew myself in You, and rest in You . . . as you fill me each day with the indwelling of Yourself. Amen.

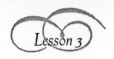

LOVE IS REAL AND PRACTICAL

"The Lord Almighty is with us"(Psalm 46:7).

The most practical thing you can do is to learn about God and seek to understand how He desires a real, practical, and personal relationship with you. God is not far off, removed from your life and unconcerned. The God of Scripture is a God who related to people in very real ways.

When we reduce God's love to a bumper sticker slogan, we miss the meaning of this very real and everyday practical relationship we can have with God. He is present with us, and we can experience Him fully.

> The word *love* has fallen on bad times. To many people it means nothing more nor less than going to bed with somebody, never mind what sex the other may belong to. Bumper stickers substitute a picture of a red heart for the word love and apply it to just about anything, anybody, or any place. In some Christian gatherings people are asked to turn around and look the person next to them full in the face, even if he is a perfect stranger, and say with a broad smile and without the least trace of a blush, "God loves you, and so do I."[1]—*Elisabeth Elliot*

It's easy to see why so many are asking, "What's love got to do with God?" Love has been neutralized, watered down, and cheapened by the culture we live in. Yet, love has everything to do with God. Why would we want to water down the power and truth of something so real and beautiful and toss it aside? Perhaps because it doesn't seem real or practical enough for our everyday realities.

Let me tell you something—Jesus Christ is the most practical and personal everyday reality you will ever come to know. God the Father sent His Son Jesus in a "real" form—the reality of flesh—for men to see, follow, and believe in. His testimony has lasted throughout the ages. The realness of Jesus Christ was God in the flesh for our ultimate salvation and deliverance. Our God is not only mighty, full of wisdom and strength, but He is also real and at work in the real things that fill up our lives.

God is like the great conductor of our lives. He is orchestrating each note in the music of our personal journey. At this very moment, God is at work. It is a tragedy that we have a deep longing to know God and experience His Love, yet we are unable to recognize Him and His love even though He embraces us in His love day after day. Far too often we attribute God's work to circumstance or coincidence rather than admitting that God is fitting all the pieces of our lives together.

Take a puzzle and empty out the box. Look at all those little pieces with various shapes, sizes, and color. To me it just looks like a heap of pieces, a mess to untangle. That is how the pieces of our lives sometimes look to us. They don't seem to make sense. Sometimes we are handed a piece that is misshapen and discolored. We can not imagine how this ugly piece can fit into the picture. Yet, we must remember that God's ways are not our ways. His ways are higher and His ways are always right. He is putting the picture together. He is placing the high notes and the low notes in harmonizing order. He is always working according to plan . . . His plan.

1. Write out Psalm 138:8.

∽ According to this verse, what will the Lord do for you?

∽ Look up the word fulfill and write down the definition.

∞ What does "the Lord will fulfill his purpose for me" mean to you?

I am encouraged by the fact that God carries out His plans for my life. I find that this is personal and enables me to trust Him in tangible ways. This truth makes me secure. When things in my personal life were splintered and shattered, I held on to this verse. It was my promise. Despite what I could see, God was fulfilling His purposes for me. Despite the ugly, misshapen pieces I was handed, God was never going to abandon the work of His hand—me.

Now as I prepare for my oldest son to go off to college, it is an amazing comfort to know that God will fulfill His purpose for my son. As much as I think I love my children, God loves them more. He will not abandon the works of His hands. What hope and joy this brings to me. I can apply this to my life every day in real and practical ways! I can encourage my son with the Scriptures and pass on to him truth to embrace, truth to find hope in, and a solid foundation on which to trust.

∞ Read the following verses and summarize how each relationship with the Lord was practical and personal. What do you see in these interactions with God that can be applied to your own life though your circumstances are different?

ADAM AND EVE: GENESIS 3:20-21
Summary:

Application:

HAGAR: GENESIS 16:1-13
Summary:

Application:

SOLOMON: 1 KINGS 3:5-13
Summary:

Application:

3. Read the following verses and summarize how each person experienced God's deliverance, power, and authority. (Be sure to notice God's obvious care about practicality and details.)

THE DISCIPLES: MARK 6:7-13

PAUL: 2 CORINTHIANS 12:7-10

PETER: ACTS 12:1-17

JOHN: REVELATION 1:9-20

4. Write out Hebrews 13:8.

∽ What does this verse say to you about Jesus Christ?

∽ If God has worked in people's lives throughout the ages, do you believe He can still work in your life today, or do you believe your life is too complex for Him to relate to your problems? Explain.

5. Read Matthew 6:25-34. How do these verses show that Jesus was practical in His dealings with people?

∽ Journal your thoughts on Matthew 6:25-34 or rewrite the passage, personalizing it in your own words.

∽ According to Matthew 6:25-34, what practical things are you not to worry about?

6. What does Jesus say about you in Matthew 6:26?

I encourage you to believe the truth that you are valuable to God!

∽ What does Matthew 6:28-32 say to you about the practical and personal side of God?

∽ In Mathew 6:31-32, what does your Heavenly Father know?

Can you grasp with me that the God of the
Universe, the Alpha and Omega, the Creator of
all things knows us in such a personal way that He
knows what is necessary, useful, and desirable in
our lives?

Need:
•something necessary
•something useful
•something desirable

God certainly knew how to reassure and help Moses. In Exodus 3:11 we
read that Moses couldn't understand why God would choose someone like
himself. He said to God, "Who am I, that I should go to Pharaoh and bring
the Israelites out of Egypt?"

God answered him with the practical truth of the situation, "I will be
with you" (Exodus 3:12).

Moses, still trying to comprehend what was happening, asked God,
"Suppose I go to the Israelites and say to them, 'The God of your fathers
has sent me to you,' and they ask me, 'What is his name?' Then what shall
I tell them?" (Exodus 3:13).

God answered Moses simply, "I AM WHO I AM" (Exodus 3:14).

God's name, I AM, says much about the realness and practical side of
God. For in that name is everything that we will ever need. He is the answer
to our problems, the healer of our hearts, the joy of our souls, the designer
of our lives. He is who He said He is, and He will be with us. This is not
only real, it is practical.

You wouldn't think of sending children out into the dark, cold night
alone. This would not be a practical thing to do. The wise and practical
thing would be to send someone with them—someone strong, wise, and
safe. Like the loving Father He is, God has not sent us out alone. He is with
us always. Jesus told His disciples before his death: "I will not leave you as
orphans; I will come to you. Before long, the world will not see me anymore, but you will see me. Because I live, you also will live. On that day you
will *realize* that I am in my Father, and you are in me, and I am in you"
(John 14: 18-20, italics added).

God knows everything we need, and He can provide it for us. If we don't
have something, we must not really need it in our lives at this time. He is in
us. He works within us. And He is "I Am" to each of us.

7. Read Matthew 6:5-8. What do these verses say about God knowing you, especially His practical involvement in your life?

The most practical thing you can do is to have a God-centered life. From this position you can experience and know the love of God on a daily basis. This is contrary to the wisdom of the world that we live in. The focus of the Bible is on God. The focus of much of the self-help materials on the market is "self." You have a choice. You must decide whether you will live a God-centered life or a self-centered life. The whole concept behind salvation is dying to self. In order to know and experience the love of God, we must come to a denial of self and develop a God-centered heart.

8. Read Deuteronomy 30:19-20. Record your thoughts of how the following directives relate to you personally. Why should we follow them?
   • Choose life.

   • Love the Lord your God.

   • Listen to His voice.

   • Hold fast to Him.

9. But . . . what if you blow it? Write out the following verses:
   • 1 John 1:9

   • Acts 10:43

- Ephesians 1:7

Redemption is when someone redeems something, buying it back or recovering it.

Do you need to be redeemed? Do you need to be recovered from past sins, present fears, and future anxieties? Well . . . good and practical news! Because of God's love, you have been redeemed by the blood of Jesus Christ. His blood purchased you—bought you back—so that you would be His forever.

I know that my Redeemer lives, and that in the end he will stand upon the earth. And after my skin has been destroyed, yet in my flesh I will see God; I myself will see him with my own eyes— I, and not another. How my heart yearns within me! (Job 19:25–27).

☙ Write out Psalm 130:7-8. Substitute your name for the name Israel.

☙ Write out Colossians 1:14.

Do you need forgiveness today? Forgiveness is an aspect of God's love that is real and practical. Each day it is important that we ask God to cleanse us from all sin and anything that would get in the way of our relationship with Him. Jesus Christ has paved the way for forgiveness. We shouldn't think of forgiveness only in terms of the "biggies"— the big sins—rather we should think of forgiveness in terms of all of our "stuff." Do you know what I mean? I have never met a woman without "stuff." So, fess up and be cleansed by the blood of Jesus. His forgiveness is an awesome and wonderful grace that does the miraculous work of an eraser on the sin in our lives.

10. Write out Philippians 2:13.

∞ According to Philippians 2:13, who is working in you?

∞ What is the purpose of His working?

If you stay God-centered, you will be allowing God to work actively in you. When you see things happen around you, you will become excited about what He is doing in and through you. You will experience Him working in your life in the most practical of ways.

So how do we enter into a "heart" relationship with God? The following verses give us guidelines.

11. **Start out the day choosing Him.** (Read the verses and journal what they mean to you.)
    • Deuteronomy 30:19-20

    • Joshua 24:15

    • Matthew 6:33

12. **Love Him through obedience** (Read the verses and journal what they mean to you.)
    • John 14:15, 24

    • John 15:10

- 1 John 2:3-6

13. **Listen to His voice** (Read the verses and journal what they mean to you.)
    - John 10:2-4

    - John 14:17

    - 1 Corinthians 2:14-15

    - Ephesians 6:17

14. **Hold fast to Him** (Read the verses and journal what they mean to you.)
    - Hebrews 10: 35-39

    - Hebrews 11:6

    - Hebrews 12:1-3

15. Write out Joshua 24:23-24.

Is any of this real and practical to you? Allowing God to become a practical part of your everyday life is what the Bible and biblical principles are all about. Too many times we pick and choose what we want to obey and believe, thus developing our own brand of "relationship." We then wonder why we feel no different about life than our unbelieving friends. A woman who is walking with God should be different. I am not talking about a difference that is measured by a set of good works. I am talking about a difference that is regulated in her heart. Who is she? What does she stand for? Is her God real, or is He just a God of nice thoughts and flowery proposals?

> *God's love meets us where the rubber meets the road in our lives. This kind of love is real and practical!*

God is real, He is powerful, and He is practical. Ask Him by the power of His Holy Spirit to show you the reality of His presence in your everyday life this week. Be prepared to share something practical, powerful, or real that God has done in any area of your life.

When Mother Teresa received her Nobel Prize, someone asked her, "What can we do to promote world peace?" She replied, "Go home and love your family."

God moves us practically doesn't He? He told Moses to go and lead the children of Israel; He told Noah to build an Ark; He told Paul to trust in the strength of God. What is He telling you to do today?

Get Christ Himself in the focus of your heart and keep Him there continually. Only in Christ will you find complete fulfillment. Throw your heart open to the Holy Spirit and invite Him to fill you. He will do it. Let no one interpret the Scriptures for you in such a way as to rule out the Father's gift of the Spirit. Every man is as full of the Spirit as he wants to be. Make your heart a vacuum and the Spirit will rush in to fill it.[2] —*A. W. Tozer*

"Come near to God and he will come near to you" (James 4:8).

"In all your ways acknowledge him, and he will make your paths straight" (Proverbs 3:6).

"The Lord Almighty is with us" (Psalm 46:7).

Dear Lord,

Come and fill me with Yourself, make me completely Yours. Anoint me each day for that day's steps. Guide me . . . step by step . . . in this journey of life. May I always see You, look for You in everything and everyone. I desire to be Your vessel, and a woman whom You can use, by the power of the Spirit of God at work within me. Thank You for redeeming me, and now I will trust in You, my Redeemer who lives! Amen.

LOVE CREATED ME

"All things were created by him and for him"(Col. 1:16).

It is easy to forget where our true roots are. "In the beginning God created. . . ." Many of us grew up relating our beginnings to two lovestruck people we learned to call our parents. Some of us grew up relating our beginnings to a mistake or an accident by two people who didn't really welcome our arrival into the world. We have forgotten that even though it takes two people to perform the physical act that can lead to a pregnancy, only God can create the miracle of life within the womb. God does not create mistakes. Your life is a miracle of God's design.

I know only too well how hard it can be to conceive a child. Longing to be a mother, I was one of those temperature-taking, month-charting women who spent a few years desperately trying to plan intimacy at the exact right time. I wanted so much to become pregnant and have a child that I bought the books and kits and followed all the "time line" rules.

Originally, I assumed it would be easy. You just get pregnant, right? Wrong! Though I did all the proper things according to the latest fertility book, I was not conceiving. Finally, after what seemed like forever, in what I now know was God's perfect timing, I conceived my first child. Even though we were doing all the "right" things, the element missing was God's perfect timing for His plan to be completed and "His" child to be born. Life is not an accident! It is ordained by God. Try as I might, I could not make it happen one day earlier than planned by God.

Like most women I experience great joy when I see little babies. I *ooh* and *aah* over each intricate little feature from head to toe. A new life has such promise to it. A new life is like a clean slate, a new beginning, something new and beautiful entering the world. Once this new little person enters the scene, nothing will ever be exactly as it was before.

So it is with you! Once you entered the scene nothing was ever the same again! You were the one that people *oohed* and *aahed* over. They scrutinized all your little features to see just whom you looked like, and they saw all the promise of tomorrow in your birth. It is easy for us to recognize the promise and miracle of life in a newborn, but what about stopping right now to recognize the promise and miracle of your life? Rejoice in the day God created you!

1. **Read Psalm 139 verses 1-17. Underline the verses that speak to your heart about your beginnings. Write out your favorite verse.**

∞ Fill in the following:

My Birth Name _____

Date of Birth _____

2. **Write out Psalm 139:13.**

∞ According to Psalm 139:13, who created you?

∞ What was happening in your mother's womb?

∞ Look up the definition of *knit* and write it here.

3. **Write out Psalm 119:73.**

∞ According to Psalm 119:73, whose hands formed you?

4. Write out Genesis 1:27.

∞ In whose image were you created?

∞ How do you usually view yourself?

∞ How does viewing yourself negatively drag you down?

The way some of us view ourselves is definitely a problem today. Not many women feel good about themselves. And, given the media pressure of the culture we live in, it is no wonder we struggle with the image we have of ourselves. All around us there are images painted of women that are without flaw, according to the world's standard.

Even though we are Christians, we still tend to measure ourselves against the images before us. Measuring ourselves with the yardstick of the world's standard is like measuring ourselves with a broken ruler . . . we will never be able to get an accurate measurement. We will always be lacking because the tool with which we measured ourselves is not accurate; however, when we measure ourselves with the ruler of God's Word, we will be measuring ourselves accurately every time. Unfortunately, even Christian women fail to look to God's measuring system for the foundation of security for which they long.

It is easy to get caught up in feeling worthless. It is not uncommon for us to feel as if we are real nobodies when we fail to achieve in any given area. When we feel worthless, we act worthless. Instead of faith ruling our lives, insecurity rules our thoughts and actions. We perceive ourselves a certain way, and then we act out those perceptions. Some call this living by a perceived identity. Clearly, our actions, attitudes, choices, and responses to life are all affected by how we view ourselves. Sadly, since most of us have an inaccurate, unbiblical view of ourselves, we act out in ways that are contrary to God's design for us.

The answer to this dilemma is seeing ourselves as God's loved and accepted children. When we see ourselves as God's children, we will live as His. When we perceive our life has value, we will live according to that value system. We need to ask God to change our perceived identity and give us our true identity, according to His Word.

5. **Read Genesis 2:7. According to this verse, who gave you your first breath?**

How easy it is for us to think of a baby's first breath as just a response to the doctor's spank on the baby's bottom. The child comes out, the doctor clears the nasal passages, holds the child upside down, and then with a little pat, out comes the bellowing cry of the newborn. Babies are born every day. The birthing procedures have become commonplace.

In the fast pace of life, sometimes we take for granted the miracles of life. Maybe you weren't tempted to take all the details of your own child's, or loved one's, birth for granted, but what about your life, your birth? What about the fact that God breathed into you the breath of life and you became a living person? Does that mean anything to you?

Most of us take for granted that we are alive. But we must remember that life is a gift and it is valuable to God. Our lives have purpose and value and will continue to have purpose and value until He allows the breath of life to cease.

∞ What would be a godly response to all of this?

6. **Write out Psalm 139:14.**

∞ What are the two words used in Psalm 139:14 to describe how you were made?

1)

2)

∞ What is the word used in this verse to describe God's works?

∞ How did David indicate that he understood this concept?

Unfortunately, not many women know full well that they are a wonderful work of God's hand. If we did know that, we would live differently. We would feel differently about ourselves, our futures, and our lives. Sadly, we get trapped in the same way unbelievers might get trapped . . . in our pasts, in our inadequacies, and especially in looking only at "appearances and achievements." These are some of the things that drag us down and keep us from experiencing God the way we would like to. We most definitely need to have our minds renewed!

7. Write out Romans 12:1-2.

∞ According to Romans 12:1-2, why should you present your life to God?

∞ Read Colossians 1:16. According to this verse, who created you?

∞ As stated in this verse, why were you created?

∞ Do you think it is reasonable for God to want you to submit your life to Him as you are instructed to in Romans 12:1? Why or why not?

8. **Instead of being fashioned after the world and its patterns, for what are you supposed to reach?**

∞ How can you apply "Do not conform any longer to the pattern of this world" to how you view yourself?

∞ Look up *transformed* in the dictionary. Write the meaning here.

∞ Look up *renew* in the dictionary and a thesaurus. Write the meaning here.

∞ How do these descriptions give you a picture of what can happen in your mind when you are renewed in the truths of God's Word?

Some of us have had a negative or less than God-inspired pattern of thinking built into us over the years. This patterning may affect several areas. The foundational issue we need to address in this journey of learning God's love is the area of how we view ourselves. Negative thoughts and self-defeating patterns are contrary to the knowledge of God.

9. **Write out 2 Corinthians 10:5.**

∞ What does this verse tell you to do with your thoughts?

∽ What are some of the thoughts you have struggled with about "you"?

Ralph Waldo Emerson said, " A man is what he thinks about all day long." Marcus Aurelius said, " A man's life is what his thoughts make it." Norman Vincent Peale says, "Change your thoughts and you change your world." The Bible says, "For as he thinketh in his heart, so is he" (Proverbs 23:7, KJV).

The Bible gives us the truth by which to pattern our thinking. When we become saturated with this new way of thinking, we will have a new way of life as well. The power of the Bible is not just in reading it or memorizing the words. The power of the Bible comes when we begin to think biblical thoughts. That's what meditating on the Word is all about—not just reading and memorizing, but reflecting, thinking, chewing on the words as if they were our own personal message from God. After all, *it is truly our personal message from God!*

I like to think of studying the Bible as marinating in the truth. I soak in it, letting it flavor who I am, seasoning who I become, and tenderizing all the tough spots in my heart. I don't have to understand everything about God's Word in order for it to work on my life; I just have to know that it does work and it does change me from the inside out.

10. Read 2 Timothy 3:16. What does this verse say to you about God's Word?

∽ Write out Hebrews 4:12.

Wow, the Word of God goes deep, doesn't it? It goes so deep that it can expose the thoughts and attitudes of our hearts. We all need that kind of probing and realigning. Next time you feel a negative attack coming on, hold up what you are thinking about yourself to the Word of Truth. How does it compare? What is real and true, no matter what you see or feel?

11. Write out Revelation 4:11.

⌘ According to the fact that God created you, do you think that He esteems you and your life as important and valuable? Why or why not?

Everybody suffers when we do not realize our personal worth.

1. *We suffer.* We aren't free to express our love, uniqueness, and gifts.

2. *Others suffer.* The way we feel about ourselves affects the way we relate to others.

Accepting the fact that you are loved and valuable is essential. Be transformed by the renewing of your mind!

12. Read Psalm 139 again. This time read it out loud, slowly and deliberately. Let God's thoughts toward you and His involvement in your life sink in a little deeper.

⌘ Now . . . write out every FACT that you find in Psalm 139 that expresses God's knowledge of you, or His love for you.

VERSE	TRUTH
1. (write out verse)	He knows me.

13. Read Ephesians 4:29-30. What does this verse have to say about your "self-talk" and how you put yourself down?

A healthy, positive self-esteem is not attained by "feel good" superficiality. On the other hand, a Christ-centered view of ourselves is not detrimental to true discipleship; it is the result of understanding and applying the truths of the Scriptures. A proper view of God and of ourselves enables us to love, obey and honor Christ with full hearts.[1]—*Robert McGee*

14. Write out Philippians 1:6.

Remember, God created you. He created you in love because He values you. The Bible says that everything God creates is good and for a purpose (1 Timothy 4:4). Because of this, you don't have to compare yourself with others ever again. Each woman is unique and individual. God's plan for each of us is different. He isn't making cookie-cutter Christians . . . it's our involvement and immaturity that produces copycat people. Each one of us has a part in God's plan. His plan is to conform us more into His image and draw us close to Himself. We make it so hard, but He didn't make it as complex as we do. He told us to believe in Him, love Him, abide in Him, and love others. Let us do just that!

- Believe God is intimately concerned with you, your soul, and your eternal future.
- Love God as a response to understanding His great love for you.
- Abide in Him, connecting to Him each morning for power and strength.
- Love others, for they too were created in the image of God, for His purposes.

Jewels in the Lord's Crown

Women are precious jewels to the Lord.
Some of us are sapphires bold and brilliant,
filled with the power of God's love.
While some are rubies filled with the energy and enthusiasm,
to share God's love.
Others are topaz warm and merciful,
in their commitment to those lives they touch for God.
Those who are amethyst are quiet and gentle,
lifting the people they meet in prayer.
And others are diamonds strong and powerful,
in their desire to draw the unsaved to the Lord.
As we intertwine to form a crown to lay before the Lord,
He rejoices not in the brilliance or the value of the jewels,
but in the love that binds our hearts together.
Donna Burke

∞ Choose the verse of Scripture that meant the most to you this week and write it on a 3x5 index card. Carry it with you each day this week. Read it often as you strive to think God's thoughts.

Go through your old pictures and find a childhood picture of yourself. Share this picture with the women in your fellowship group. If you aren't doing this study with other women, then just get the picture out for yourself. Reflect on who God created when He put you together in your mother's womb. Look at the picture several times this week. Perhaps you can even use it, for just this week, as a bookmark in your Bible. Each time you look at that picture, tell yourself, "*God created me!*"

Though outwardly we are wasting away, yet inwardly we are being renewed day by day. So we fix our eyes not on what is seen, but on what is unseen. For what is seen is temporary, but what is unseen is eternal (2 Corinthians 4:16, 18).

Know therefore that the Lord your God is God; he is the faithful God, keeping his covenant of love to a thousand generations of those who love him and keep his commands (Deuteronomy 7:9).

Dear Lord,

Forgive me for all the times I have taken life for granted. You have given me life and breath. I have neglected to thank You for who I am and who You are faithfully forming me to be. I look at the negative, You dwell on the positive. I look at impossible, You look at possibilities. I want more than anything to be renewed in my mind and changed in my thinking. Make this a reality in my life, as I marinate in Your Word, soaking in all that is true about me…in You. Amen.

LOVE ORDAINS MY DAYS

"All the days ordained for me were written in your book before one of them came to be" (Psalm 139:16).

I can remember wondering what I would be when I actually grew up. Thoughts of the perfect life began to fill my mind at a young age, and unrealistic expectations shaped my dreams of the future. On occasion my mother would sing this song to me:

> When I was just a little girl,
> I asked my mother what would I be
> Will I be pretty? Will I be rich?
> Here's what she said to me.
> "Que Sera Sera, Whatever will be, will be
> The future's not ours to see
> Que Sera Sera."

Here I am today, grown up, and still wondering at times, "Lord, what am I going to be?" or more accurately, *"Lord, who am I and where am I going?"* We all would like to know the future, or at least we think we would like to know it. I take great comfort in knowing that God has planned my days—the length of them, and the breadth of them.

1. **Write out Psalm 139:16.**

This is one of my favorite verses. It gives me great confidence and peace. When this truth sinks deep within my very soul, I can then have a new perspective of my life and be more patient with the overall plan—the big picture. When God corrects me, deals with me, or allows things to cross my path, I have the hope that He knows exactly what shape my life is supposed to take and that He will be the faithful power at work within me to mold me into the woman He has designed for me to be.

Notice here that Psalm 139:16 doesn't say **some** of my days, but **ALL MY DAYS**. Have you had days that didn't add up in your mind to the love of God?

(I don't know about you, but sometimes something as small as a bad hair day can really set me off. That is, until I get a grip and begin praising God in the midst of everything, everyday, always!) Life is not always a joy ride. Some seasons are very hard. That is why we need the hope of knowing that our life is in His hand . . . always has been, always will be.

> Wherever we find ourselves, God has a reason for placing us there. He has His hand upon our lives and upon each circumstance in our lives. We may be going through difficult trials, but hardships are necessary. God wants to develop in us the characteristics that will enable us to fulfill His plan for us. God is working in each of us.[1]—*Chuck Smith*

He has ordained my days. Ordain:
•to set forth expressly and with authority;
•to dictate;
•to put in order;
•to establish by appointment;
•to prescribe;
•to call the shots;
•to tune;
•to lay it on the line.

How exciting to realize that God is putting my life in order. He is setting up divine appointments that bring forth His will in my life. He is calling the shots and fine-tuning each part of me for His glory. And it is all happening through circumstances He has planned for me to encounter.

2. **Write out 1 Peter 2:9.**

What does 1 Peter 2:9 mean to you?

∞ For what do you think you are chosen?

3. Write out Ephesians 2:10.

The Greek word for workmanship is *poiema*. This word means masterpiece, work of art, poem. The bottom line is this: you are His work, His poetry, His expression, His masterpiece. This is the truth about you. God will work in you by His grace and power so that He might accomplish the plan He has for you, for His kingdom and for His glory.

∞ What is the result of being chosen by God?

∞ Who prepared good works for your life in advance?

4. Write out Colossians 1:16.

By Him and for Him. Those few words now give new meaning to my life. They are my personal slogan. They explain what I live for and who I live for. My unspoken slogan used to be *by me and for me.* Everything was always just about me. What does Debbie want? . . . Instead of What would Jesus do? But, those words—*by Him and for Him*—simplify my purpose and meaning. They simplify my choices and help me focus on what is important.

5. Write out Jeremiah 1:5.

You were created by God, and created for His purposes! Before you were born, He set you apart. Think about that. Next time you are tempted to

Purpose:
•what one intends to do or achieve;
•the proper activity of a person;
•to have in mind a goal;
•to have aim, and meaning.

think your life doesn't have any purpose . . . don't go there! Instead, go to the Word of God and drink in the truth of His purpose—by Him and for Him.

God has set us apart for His purposes. He knows what He intends to do, and He knows the proper activity that suits us expressly, according to His design of who we are as individuals. Knowing that He has ordained our days gives us purpose and meaning. Knowing that He planned for us gives us vision for the future and for all that He has intended for us.

You Dreamed Me Up

O dear God, it was You, You alone who dreamed me up.
Nobody else would ever have thought of me
or planned for me,
or looked right through me with future contemplation.
Right from the beginning of time I was all your idea.
You had big things in mind for me, good things,
glorious things.
And now, with magnificent dexterity you are making
them come to pass.
And I? Well, I stand amazed on the sideline and praise
your infinite patience.
Ruth Harms Calkin[2]

6. **Write out Luke 19:10.**

7. **Read Matthew 4:19 and Matthew 28:18-20. In what will you eventually become involved, according to these verses?**

God's purpose is to save the lost and restore lives. God created each of us for His purpose. Within each of us are genetics and characteristics that make us unique and individual women. God loves us and calls us His wonderful work. He takes joy in using us for His Glory. His desire for our lives is that we would bring praise, glory, and honor to Him.

Do you have to be an evangelist, saving thousands, to bring glory to God? No. You need to be "you." If part of being "you" is evangelistic, then *go for it*. But, if being "you" is serving meals to the needy, then serve them with a smile and with all your heart. If "you" is helping someone decorate her home, adding beauty and peace to her environment, then do it with flair and joy!

Whatever you do, do that very thing unto the Lord, whether it is changing diapers, driving carpools, running corporate meetings, cooking for your family, being there for your friends, or sharing the Gospel. Do all for the glory of God!

∽ What was Jesus' goal in coming to this earth?

It is God's goal to bring people to a love relationship with Jesus Christ. A relationship where we remain in Him, renew ourselves in Him, and rest in Him. As we begin to understand that His love involves using us in all the circumstances we find ourselves in, we begin to get excited about the prospect of being used by God.

We are being made into everyday vessels through which God can pour each day. Unlike a fragile china teapot, we will become strong and durable. A special little pot that requires special handling only gets taken off the shelf for special occasions—not so for the strong and durable everyday vessel. We are being made strong, secure, and durable for God's purposes each day. This happens as we get into the Word of God and learn more about who God is and what His plan is.

You shouldn't wait for a special occasion to be open to God's use. Start today. Remember that He has plans that are being carried out right this moment.

8. Read Romans 8:28-30. Think about these verses and jot down thoughts on the facts below.

- God works for the good in all things.

- I am called according to His purpose.

- God foreknew me. (He called me from my mother's womb.)

- God predestined me to be conformed to the likeness of His Son (changed from the inside out).

- God called me.

- God justified me.

- God glorified me. (Christ in us is the hope of glory.)

It is only a faithful person who truly believes that God sover-eignly controls his circumstances. We take our circumstances for granted, saying God is in control, but not really believing it. We act as if the things that happen were completely controlled by people. To be faithful in every circumstance means that we have only one loyalty, or object of our faith— the Lord Jesus Christ. God may cause our circumstances to suddenly fall apart, which may bring the realization of our unfaithfulness to Him for not recognizing that He had ordained the situation. We never saw what He was trying to accomplish, and that exact event will never be repeated in our life. This is where the test of our faith-fulness comes. If we will just learn to worship God even during the difficult circumstances, He will change them for the better very quickly if He so chooses.[3] —*Oswald Chambers*

9. **Finish reading the rest of Romans 8. According to these verses, who is for you?**

∞ Who is interceding for you?

∞ What can separate you from the love of Christ?

Romans chapter 8 is incredibly powerful. You should read it over and over again. Let it sink into your thoughts, trickling down into your heart, and changing your perspective.

Knowing that God created you, chose you, and has your days mapped out can give you a wonderful new perspective. It is exciting to think that God is in control. Even control freaks can learn to take comfort in the fact that God is in control and nothing can separate you from Him and His love for you.

His love for us is the motivating factor in all He does. Love is who He is. Love is His nature. We can have victory in our hardships and victory in

It is quite trendy to get yourself together and get on a spiritual path. A spiritual path to where? It is all vague and uncertain. Get spiritual, be the best you can be, you only have one life to live . . .

our triumphs because of the love of God. Paul says we are more than conquerors through Him who loved us

Don't yawn! Don't fall asleep! Don't just think *here we go with that love stuff again.* Over and over we read of the love of God. Yet, over and over again we take it for granted and do not acknowledge that it is a powerful force in our lives, ordaining our days, and giving us purpose. Embracing His steadfast love can change your life. It is changing mine daily!

10. Read Romans 9:16.

∞ According to Romans 9:16, on what does God's work depend?

∞ Is it influenced by your effort?

∞ Read on to Romans 9:17. Do you think it is clear that God has purposes for everything He created? Why or why not?

11. Read Esther 4:12-14.

God raised Esther up, making her the wife of a king so that at the proper time she would have an influence in sparing the Jewish people. It is clear that God raised her up for that point in time. He completed His will through her.

∞ Do you think God ordained her position for a specific time and purpose? Why or why not?

∞ Write out Psalm 4:3.

12. Read Psalm 20.

Often we do not understand the purpose of the situations in our lives. It is in these times especially that we should put all our trust in the name of the Lord our God. We need to ask for His direction and praise Him that He has everything in His hand. And, by His power He will move in our lives.

∞ Write out Psalm 21:7. Personalize this verse by putting your name in the place of the word king.

It a wonderful trait to be secure and not to be shaken. We can be! We can be so confident in God, and in the FACT that He is a sovereign God always working in us the purposes of His will, that we are not shaken by any circumstance.

13. Write out Psalm 22:5.

∞ Write out Psalm 22:9-10.

14. Read Psalm 139:17-18.

In Psalm 139 we read that God's thoughts toward us are more in number than the grains of sand. Have you ever actually tried counting sand? I tried it one day. It was impossible. To me this is a beautiful picture of how it is impossible to count the thoughts God has of me. He has plans, He has intentions, and He is always thinking of me. Thank God that it is He who fashioned my days! Next time you have your child, grandchild, or friend at the park or beach, pick up a handful of sand. Let it slip through your fingers and see for yourself.

15. Jot down the key words in the following verses and your thoughts on each.

- Proverbs 19:21-22

- Proverbs 20:24

- Proverbs 21:30

- Ecclesiastes 3:11

Many are the plans in a [woman's] heart, but it is the Lord's purpose that prevails. What a [woman] desires is unfailing love (Proverbs 19:21-22).

God ordains compassion and love toward me.

I wrote a song for a friend of mine in 1980. As a young adult, she was my very first friend to have a baby. So, when I saw my friend's beautiful new daughter, the reality of the magnificent miracle of God's creative work swept over me.

I was completely taken by the beauty and the miracle of life. The realization that this little girl, Micah, was planned by God became very real to me. As I thanked God for Micah's birth, I wrote this song. It later became my own sons' song as I often sang these same words that were written for Micah to Justin and Cameron. In many ways it is a song for us all because nothing could have stopped our birth. We are alive as a result of God's plan.

Micah's Song

Little baby, born today
Nothing could have stood in the way
For you are a part of God's plan.
Precious one, so soft and sweet
I hope we can teach you to sit at the feet
Of Jesus. He has a purpose just for you.
As we look at you now child
We must believe you are part of a plan
Designed by God's own hand.
His special, our special, little one.

Keep in your mind the truth that you were created by God . . . for Him. *By Him and for Him!* You are part of His plan—just believe it. He has a plan carved out just for you. Stick close to His side, so you don't miss a beat!

Remember the baby or childhood picture I asked you to take out? Have you been using it for a bookmark, or has it been in clear view this week? Well . . . guess what? I took out a picture of myself too. It is an old black- and-white photo of a four-year-old girl on top of a little pony, with a huge pout on her face. I put it in a frame that says, "Bloom where you are planted." I placed it out with all the other family pictures to remind me that not only was I created by God . . . but I am to let my roots go down deep into Him regardless of my circumstances. For surely, in all things He is at work con- forming me into His image. This is what He has ordained, set forth, pre- scribed, appointed . . . for me, His child.

The Lord will perfect that which concerns me; Your mercy and loving-kindness, O Lord, endure forever; forsake not the works of Your own hands
(Psalm 138:8, AMP).

I will cry to God Most High, Who performs on my behalf and rewards me—Who brings to pass His purposes for me and surely completes them!
(Psalm 57:2, AMP)

Dear Lord,

May I never take my life for granted. You had something in mind when You created me. You are working in me even now, molding me and shaping me, conforming me into Your image. I am grateful that I have Your Spirit, and that I have purpose beyond myself. For in You I find all things, and in You I can rest in the plans and purposes of a big God. Amen.

LOVE IS MY FOUNDATION

"Blessed are those whose strength is in you"(Psalm 84:5).

While looking up *foundation* in the dictionary, I found some descriptions that helped me understand how important a foundation is when building a relationship with a loving God. **A foundation is: a base, or the basis on which something stands.**

Every woman has a foundation just as every building has a foundation. When the foundation is weak and unstable, the entire building is unstable. It is the same for us. When our foundation is weak, we become unstable, anxious, and insecure women. On the contrary when we are being built on a firm, solid base, we will grow into firm, solid, secure women.

These days it is common to base our foundation on "self." We are encouraged, "Learn to love yourself. Trust yourself. Be strong and lean on yourself. If you believe in yourself, you can do anything."

> *We are much like the building of a new structure. Therefore, if any— one is in Christ, he is a new creation; the old has gone, the new has come!*
> *(2 Corinthians 5:17)*

While it is good to accept yourself and embrace the love God has for you, focusing on "self" is just another distraction or trap that leads us to believe in ourselves for completeness.

The Bible tells us to **believe in God** and that through His power all things are possible. The book of Proverbs tells us not to be wise in our own eyes and not to lean on our own understanding. Yet, even as Christian women we continue to rely solely on ourselves at times. The Bible may give direct instruction and wisdom in an area that we don't want to agree with, so we trust in ourselves and pick and choose whom and what we will believe. This is not building our life on a solid foundation but on very unstable ground.

As we learn to accept that we serve a loving God, we will learn that He can be absolutely trusted with our lives. It is then that we will want to build our lives on His wisdom and His Word, rejoicing in the strength and security of His foundation.

1. Read Matthew 7:24-27. Write these verses in your own words.

> These words I speak to you are not incidental additions to your life, homeowner improvements to your standard of living. They are foundational words, words to build a life on. If you work these words into your life, you are like a smart carpenter who built his house on solid rock. Rain poured down, the river flooded, a tornado hit—but nothing moved that house. It was fixed to the rock.
>
> But if you just use my words in Bible studies and don't work them into your life, you are like a stupid carpenter who built his house on the sandy beach. When a storm rolled in and the waves came up, it collapsed like a house of cards (Matthew 7:24-27, TM)

2. Write out Proverbs 14:1.

∞ If you are to be wise women, on what foundation should your house and your life be built?

∞ According to Proverbs 14:1, what will happen if you build on the wrong foundation?

∞ Have you actually purposed in your heart to believe the Bible as truth and to base your entire life on that truth as your solid foundation? Why or why not?

3. **Look up the following verses, and write key thoughts.**

   • 2 Timothy 3:16-17

   • James 1:22-25

4. **Write out Proverbs 31:25-26.**

The Bible is a record of God working mightily in and through the lives of ordinary people.
Billy Graham

∞ Why do you think the woman described in Proverbs 31:25-26 can laugh at the future?

∞ On what do you think her life is based?

∞ Look up *strength* in your dictionary. Write the definition here.

∞ Look up *dignity* in your dictionary, and write the definition here.

∞ Do you think a woman who is clothed with strength and dignity is a secure woman? Explain.

There is no better security than to have Christ as our foundation, our rock, our anchor. Then when the storms of life come—and they will—we will remain standing. Life can be tough at times, and when our foundation is self, friends, family, or things, we are on shaky and unpredictable ground.

Anything other than our relationship with God can be taken from us. That is one of the reasons that it is important to put all of our eggs into one basket—Jesus Christ. Then we can know that no matter what happens, we are solid and secure.

How many people do you know who are secure despite their circumstances? How many women do you know who can laugh at the future, especially when none of us are certain about the circumstances that will surround our futures?

If we are going to be wise women, we must build our lives not on the sands of time, but on faith in Jesus Christ and His Word. Otherwise, we will be Nervous Nellies, anxiously living through each day as if there were no God in Heaven. Too many women live like this. But ladies, good news . . . there is a God in heaven, and He cares for you!

Let a living God be your foundation. The creator of all things is willing and able to give your life the anchor and stability that it needs.

You may be asking yourself, "How do I have God as my foundation?" The answer is this: daily lay your life before God, allowing Him to then build on your surrendered heart.

The Lesson

Lord, for many months I prayed
To be filled with the Holy Spirit
That I might have more of Jesus.
But slowly you are teaching me
That to be filled with the Holy Spirit
Means that Jesus has all of me.
Ruth Harms Calkin [1]

5. Write out Romans 10:17.

Before our lives can be built securely by God, a foundation must be laid. We must have a solid, secure, strong base. In order to have the materials for this foundation, we must be in God's Word. To understand love as our foundation, we must read of His love for us and meditate on the truth.

When it comes to the major-league difficulties like death, disease, sin and disaster—you know that God cares. But what about the smaller things? What about grouchy bosses or flat tires or lost dogs? What about broken dishes, late flights, toothaches, or a crashed hard disk? Do these matter to God?

I mean, He's got a universe to run. He's got the planets to keep balanced and presidents and kings to watch over. He's got wars to worry about and famines to fix. Who am I to tell him about my ingrown toenail?

I'm glad you asked. Let me tell you who you are.

In fact, let me proclaim who you are.

You are an heir of God and a co-heir with Christ.

You are eternal, like an angel.

You have a crown that will last forever.

> You are a holy priest, a treasured possession.
>
> But more than any of the above—more significant than any title or position—is the simple fact that you are God's child."[2] —*Max Lucado*

God's child? Now that's an inheritance! If we truly believe what is true about us, and about our God, our foundation will be as firm as the strongest concrete. In fact, that is exactly what it will be like.

6. Write out Joshua 1:8.

⌒ Write out Psalm 119:9.

It is in embracing the Word of God and meditating on the truth that we tear down the negative images and messages on which we have built our lives in the past. God is all-powerful and can use even the sometimes ugly events of our pasts to help mold us into the strong, God-confident women that He has designed us to be. I emphasize being God-confident because having absolute confidence in God needs to be the firm foundation on which all else can then be securely built.

Think of a house. We are building our house on the Rock, Jesus Christ. Confidence in God is our new foundation. This leads to confidence in ourselves, the women that He is making us to be because we are in Him. And, we begin to have respect for ourselves because we realize our value and worth in His plan. These two together add up to the freedom to reach out to others in true humility and love. We become women who are no longer bound, but women who are free to be ourselves. When this freedom is a result of growing in biblical truths, then we are set free indeed.

7. Write out Ephesians 6:10.

∞ What do you think Ephesians 6:10 means?

∞ Is God's mighty power your foundation? Why or why not?

∞ Are you strong?

∞ What is the source of your strength?

∞ Write out Ephesians 6:11.

∞ According to Ephesians 6:11, what is the full armor of God?

8. **Read Ephesians 6:12-17. What are your thoughts on the following statements?**
   * We struggle.

   * We need armor.

   * The days are evil.

- We need His Word to stand.

- Take your stand against the devil's schemes.

To stand firm Jesus Christ must be our foundation!

9. **Read John 17:15-17. By what are you sanctified?**

(Note: To be sanctified means to be set apart. How exciting that God sets us apart. His Word gives us a foundation that is set apart from the secular world we live in. He gives us a peace that surpasses understanding, a joy that triumphs above our circumstances, and a love that is fixed, firm, and unchanging.)

∽ What does all this mean to you personally?

Some of us have no foundation at all. We keep trying to build on a mound of debris. We may once have had a beautiful and solid foundation, but somewhere along the way it was torn up and discarded. Perhaps you need a new foundation poured so that your life might be built on the security of Christ Jesus.

> We can forget about God. Oh, we don't stop loving God. We don't stop believing in God. But quite honestly, we forget about Him. Remember that no matter how noble or good a

certain thing is in and of itself, anything that comes between us and Jesus can become sin. We must not become so preoccupied with religious activity that we forget about Jesus. We should hate to take a single step without Him. Like Jesus, we too must be about our Father's business—and we won't manage that unless we walk with Him every moment of our lives.[3] —*Greg Laurie*

We learn to stand firm in the truth by looking at everything in light of God's Word. The Bible becomes our standard. If thoughts come to our minds that are contrary to the truth in God's Word, we must dismiss them. We must say, "No! I believe what God says about me, my life, and my future."

It is time that we live in the truth on a daily basis. It is only then that we will be set free!

∽ Think about the children's story "The Three Little Pigs." What do you remember about it?

Well, obviously there was a big bad wolf, and maybe you have had some big bad wolves in your life too. They may not be people; the wolves might be circumstances that have become so overwhelming to you that you are sure your little house will collapse at any moment. This is where the rubber meets the road. Will the hardships of life do you in? Satan certainly is set on huffing and puffing and blowing your house down! But, Jesus Christ has overcome the world and the power of Satan. Is your foundation Jesus Christ today?

10. Write out Psalm 36:7 and Psalm 36:10.

Isn't it amazing how much God loves you? You are precious to Him—that's what His Word says. He thinks about you so much that you cannot even begin to count the endless thoughts He has about you. And, you wake up each day because you are in His hands. This is a loving father, one in whom you can totally trust and rely on. His love for you must be the foundation of your life. Everything else will spring forth from this foundation of love and acceptance.

All that we build is going to be inspected by God. When God inspects us with His searching and refining fire, will He detect that we have built enterprises of our own on the foundation of Jesus? We are living in a time of tremendous enterprises, a time when we are trying to work for God, and that is where the trap is. Profoundly speaking, we can never work for God. Jesus, as the Master Builder, takes us over so that He may direct and control us completely for His enterprises and His building plans; and no one has any right to demand where He will be put to work.[4]—*Oswald Chambers*

11. Write out Psalm 119:37. I encourage you to make this verse your prayer this week

Oh, that we would be women who turn our eyes from the worthless, vain, worldly foundations that have made us insecure, weak, and fearful. May we instead fix our eyes on Jesus, the author and finisher of our faith, that we may be strong, unmovable women of God!

Dear Lord,

There are many things around me that scream for my attention. Things that seem right in themselves. But, some of these things do not lead me closer to You. In fact, some just lead me to trusting myself. Father, I do not want to base my life on "me." I want to base my life on You.

Thank You for working in me, causing me to desire You and Your strong, firm base as the security for my life. I love You! Make me now a woman of confidence, security, and strength. Do this work in me by the power of Your Holy Spirit and by the building of firm and solid foundations. Amen.

LOVE IMPARTS CONFIDENCE IN ME

". . . for the Lord will be your confidence" (Prov. 3:26).

Confidence is a quality lacking in women today. Though there are more confidence seminars than ever before, confidence is still some unattainable, unexplainable vapor in most women's lives. What is confidence? The dictionary defines it this way:

> a feeling of trust,
> faith,
> a relationship of trustful intimacy,
> fearlessness,
> self-assuredness (self-confidence),
> a feeling of certainty.

As we studied in the last lesson, building our life on sand or on an improper foundation, equals building our life on uncertainty. If the Word of God is not our foundation, we will be women tossed by every circumstance. The opposite of confidence can be explained this way:

> low self-esteem,
> fear,
> insecurity,
> lack of trust and faith.

How can God's love impart confidence in us? Let's apply His Word to the above definitions of confidence.

A Feeling of Trust

This comes as we see God's faithfulness to us and to others as written in His Word. We begin to get the picture that He is a Loving Father and that we can trust Him. We begin to see the pattern of how He worked in and through people's lives, weaving His faithfulness in and out of each event with absolute purpose.

Faith

This comes by building ourselves up with the promises of His Word (faith comes by hearing the Word of God). We see that He has been faithful to His people from generation to generation. His love won't stop now! We can apply His words and His faithfulness to our lives on a personal level.

> Faith makes the Uplook Good
> The Outlook Bright
> The Inlook Favorable
> And the Future Glorious.[1]—*Barbara Johnson*

A Relationship of Trustful Intimacy

Trustful intimacy comes as we develop a personal relationship with God. This is the daily connecting to the vine and depending-on-God type of life. Personal relationship involves TIME. It involves talking to God, thanking God, obeying His Word, and . . . being up close and personal with Him!

> All of us can know Him in this deeper sense. All of us have the unbelievable privilege of walking with the Lord of the Universe, of talking with Him daily, of asking Him to guide us, and expecting Him to enter into every facet of our lives. It's Jesus Christ Himself who invites you to look deeply into His loving eyes and take firm hold of His strong hands. He wants to keep you company as you walk through all of life.[2]—*Greg Laurie*

Fearlessness

This comes by building ourselves up with His Word that declares His love for us. If God is for us, who can be against us?! His Word talks of His loving protection over and over. We need to realize that our lives are actually in His hands and in His keeping. It is His nature to lovingly care for us. When we know these things, we grow in confidence and security and move a step away from fear.

> We are afraid that the God who says He loves us will prove in the end to be more demanding than loving. I am convinced that the real reason we pray so little is fear: fear of facing God, fear also of facing our own and others' brokenness. I think our fearful hearts are saying: "Can I really trust God? Will He really show me His love when I don't keep anything hidden from Him?"[3] —*Henri J. M. Nouwen*

As we begin to grasp His love for us, fear will become less of an issue in our lives. We will begin to realize that we can be real with our issues, our feelings, and our struggles. We will have confidence to trust in a loving, faithful God.

Self-assuredness (self-confidence)

This comes as we learn who we are in Christ. We learn we have value and a place in this world, but that apart from God, we can accomplish nothing of eternal value. Our confidence soars as we realize that in Him all things are possible, and we are in Him! It is the "I can do all things through Him who gives me the strength and ability" kind of confidence. 1 Corinthians 1:31 states: "Let him who boasts boast in the Lord." This is God-confidence—acceptance of self, based on belief in God.

A Feeling of Certainty

This is that sense of knowing God's love and provision. It comes by meditating on His Word and letting His Word sink into every pore and fiber of your being. It is an amazing peace and confidence that comes from being certain you are loved and that your life is "Father-filtered."

All of the above add up to confidence in a sovereign, loving God who operates in grace and mercy! We grow in confidence as we grow in an understanding of who He really is.

1. **Write out Psalm 21:7, using your name in the place of king.**

2. **Write out the following verses:**

∞ Psalm 54:4.

∞ Psalm 62:11-12.

∞ Psalm 63:3-5.

∞ Psalm 139:5.

Think about Psalm 139:5. Really think about what it is saying for a moment. Imagine that the Lord goes before you and behind you and then lays His hand on you, as if to seal you. Isn't it wonderful to think of a God who encompasses us with Himself? Psalm 139:6 says that the very thought of this is too much to understand, and the rest of the psalm goes on to explain how God is always with us.

3. Read Psalm 139:6-12. What kind of picture do you see here of God and His care for you?

∞ Does reading these verses build your confidence? How?

For many of us confidence is a struggle. Years of insecurity and fear keep us always at arm's length from God. This hinders our ability to have confidence in Him and His love for us. He wants to heal us from this pit of insecurity and low self-esteem.

∞ Why do you suppose God would want to deliver you from feeling terrible about yourself and your life?

∞ Do you think being insecure causes you to be a bit too self-focused at times? How?

∞ Does this stop you from being completely God-centered? Explain.

∞ Do your insecurities cause you to worry about pleasing people, rather than living to please God? Why or why not?

Our insecurities can cause us to do crazy things. They can cause us to act in ways that are not compatible with God's Word and certainly not pleasing to Him. Sometimes insecurities can cause us to lie, stretch truth, be overly sensitive, gossip, separate friends, act arrogantly, have unbecoming attitudes, and so on. How do we get to the bottom of these insecurities, and let God and His Word reside more richly in our hearts and minds?

We must return to Romans 12:2, and we must renew our thought patterns with the truth of God. This cannot be said enough. God's Word will do the work. The Bible says it is sharper that a two-edged sword, able to cut away at our hearts!

4. Write out Hebrews 4:12.

God means what he says. What he says goes. His powerful Word is as sharp as a surgeon's scalpel, cutting through everything, whether doubt or defense, laying us open to listen and obey. Nothing and no one is impervious to God's Word. We can't get away from it—no matter what (Hebrews 4:12, TM).

For every negative thing we hear or think, we need many more positives to counterbalance the one, single negative. This is why it is so important to fill up on God's promises. God's Word is the truth. We need to KNOW His Word and be able to recall His words in an instant.

Years ago, while in the midst of an unexpected and unwanted divorce, I felt helpless, wounded, and worthless. I suppose you could say I had no confidence at all. This feeling of failure caused me to plummet into despair to the point that I could not even grasp God. I could no longer relate to His Word or His promises to me. During that time of darkness, several verses that I had memorized over the years came back to my mind. I repeated those basic verses over and over to myself. Sometimes I would say them in the hush of sobs, and other times I would say them out loud with enthusiasm. After a short while of just repeating the Word of God to myself, my spirits began to lift and I was able to turn my focus from self-pity and back to God and His love for me.

I then began reading Psalm 139 out loud each morning. Every day I was reminding myself who my maker was, how He was watching over me, and the fact that He had fashioned my days and ordained them. All day I was filled with thoughts about the wonder of God and how His Word was healing me and lifting me up to places that I never thought I would be able to go again because of the pain of the divorce. God's Word truly can heal us from broken hearts. His Word is powerful in meeting our every need.

5. Write out Psalm 61:2.

∽ Write out Psalm 71:5-6.

As I look at Psalm 71:6, I am prompted to ask God always to be my confidence. From birth we all relied on God to keep our hearts beating and our lungs filled with air. It was an unspoken reliance, but nevertheless it was reliance for life, pure and simple. Then we grew up and many of us became so sophisticated that we forgot God and turned instead to people—parents, friends, relatives. But, because those people are imperfect humans just like us, they failed us, and we became afraid to trust anyone again. Think again . . . God can be trusted! He has kept us for many years. It was He who brought us forth out of our mother's womb, and He can be our confidence. Remember . . . Confidence in God=security.

6. Read the following verses and then write down the adjectives they use to describe God. The more you come to know of His nature, the more secure and confident you will be.

• Psalm 111:4

• Exodus 34:6-7

We need to know the truth in more than just an intellectual way. We need to allow God's truth to penetrate the most basic parts of our lives, such as our motives, goals, sense of self-worth, and our confidence. In many cases, God's love has only touched the surface and has not yet penetrated our deepest thoughts and beliefs about ourselves. Often these misbeliefs reflect misperceptions such as these:

God doesn't really care about me.

I am an unlovable, worthless person. Nobody will ever love me.

I'll never be able to change.

I've been a failure all my life. I guess I'll always be a failure.

If people really knew me, they wouldn't like me.

> When the light of love and honesty shines on thoughts of hopelessness, it is often very painful. We begin to admit that we really do feel negatively about ourselves, and have for a long time. But, God's love, expressed through His people, and woven into our lives by His Spirit and His Word can, over a period of time, bring healing even to our deepest wounds and instill within us an appropriate sense of self-worth.[4] —*Robert McGee*

7. **Read 2 Corinthians 5:14-15. According to these verses, whom are you supposed to live to please?**

8. **Write out Proverbs 3:26.**

∞ Write out Isaiah 32:17.

∞ Write out Jeremiah 17:17.

∞ Journal your thoughts today on the above verses. Who is supposed to be our confidence?

Separated from God and His Word, people have only their abilities and the opinions of others on which to base their worth, and the circumstances around them ultimately control the way they feel about themselves.[5] —*Robert McGee*

---

9. **Read Romans 1:20-25. What do the following statements have to say about our search for meaning and confidence?**
   - Although they claimed to be wise, they became fools.

   - They exchanged the truth of God for a lie.

   - They worshiped things and people rather than the creator.

Did you ever stop and think how it is so incredible that we look to others to discover our worth when their perspective is as limited and darkened as our own? We need instead to rely on God's steady uplifting Word to discover who we are and what we are worth. Ask God to help you look only to Him for approval, and ask Him to tear down the lies you have believed about yourself. **Exchange those lies for His truth!**

Understanding we have a loving God compels us to action because when we know we are loved, we want to respond to that love by living a life pleasing to Him. And as we grow in our understanding of God's nature and

His love for His people, we will grow in confidence and trust.

10. Read Psalm 136 out loud. What is the repeated theme of this psalm?

In Proverbs 23:7 (KJV) we read, " For as [she] thinketh in [her] heart, so is [she]."

From this verse in Proverbs, we can conclude that we must get to the very heart of the matter . . . our thoughts and attitudes. As Robert McGee states in his book *Search for Significance,* we have a choice. We can either continue to evaluate our worth based on the world's standards: **confidence/self-worth=performance and others opinions.**

Or we can judge our worth by God's standards: **confidence/self-worth=God's truth about me.** If we want to live our lives as God intended, we must embrace His truth as our standard and measuring tool.

11. Write out Hebrews 10:35.

Do not throw away the truth of God's Word, which can give you confidence in yourself!

This week remind yourself daily: His love endures forever.

Dear Lord,

Sometimes it is hard for me to believe that You truly love me. I look only at my circumstances, and I tend to forget about You. Please forgive me. I ask You to work in my heart, healing old hurts, teaching me through old wounds, that I might become a woman who is God-confident every day. It is a vain and foolish thing to try and boost myself up. Instead, may You be magnified in me, and may You be lifted up. Amen.

LOVE CORRECTS ME

"The Lord disciplines those he loves"(Heb.12:6).

As a parent I am constantly challenged by the fact that I am shaping lives on a daily basis. In love it is important for me to help my children, correcting them when they make mistakes and giving them confidence and wings to soar. In the same way the Lord God, as our Heavenly Father, is shaping our lives each day. In the process of shaping, He too corrects us when we are in error and gives us confidence to soar to higher places in Him. Every correction we receive from the Lord is all part of His shaping our lives into His Design.

My children love me, but they certainly don't like to be corrected. Nobody is thrilled with a restriction or a time-out. But, sometimes that is exactly what we need. Sometimes our circumstances act as a restriction for us, nudging us to look into an area of our lives with which God is dealing. Sometimes circumstances force us into a time-out, and though we don't want to sit in a chair in the corner of the room, staring at every spot on the wall, sitting there may be exactly the way God gets our attention. Once He has our attention, He can lovingly correct us.

We must keep in mind that even though God corrects us, His love never changes toward us. There were times when my children were younger that they would storm out of the room saying, "You just don't love me, Mom!" after I had corrected them. Nothing could have been farther from the truth. My love for them didn't change, it was just taking a shape that they didn't like at that moment.

God's love for us never changes. But, His love isn't always warm and fuzzy. Part of His love involves correction and discipline. In fact, Scripture says that this is one of the ways we know we are His daughters and that He loves us.

1. **The Bible often uses the word** *discipline.* **Look up the definition of** *discipline* **in your dictionary. Write it here.**

∽ Look up the definitions of *correct* and *correction* in your dictionary. Write them here.

∽ Write out Proverbs 3:11-12.

2. **Read Hebrews 12:1-13. Summarize what you think these verses are saying to you.**

> Our sufferings may be rough and hard to bear, but they teach us lessons, which in turn equip and enable us to help others. Our attitude toward suffering should not be, "Grit your teeth and bear it," hoping it will pass as quickly as possible. Rather, our goal should be to learn all we can from what we are called upon to endure.[1]—*Billy Graham*

3. Write out Hebrews 12:1.

Life is compared to a race in this verse. Read this verse again—out loud. Then journal what God is speaking to you through the following words.

- throw off everything that hinders

- the sin that so easily entangles

- let us run with perseverance

- the race marked out for us

Runners wear unbinding clothing when they are in a race. They wear nothing that will hinder their performance during the run and nothing that will stop them from reaching their goal. They also run with patience, even though there are many parts of the course that are less than thrilling. Despite what they feel, they stay focused on their goal of making it across the finish line.

∞ Do you think you could keep running a race if you had a pebble or a rock in your running shoe?

∞ Would it be wise to stop, take the rock out, lace the shoes up again, and get back on track?

∽ What rocks do you have in your life today that are hindering you? How are they keeping you from your goals?

4. **Read Hebrews 12:2. Read it again—out loud. Then journal what God is speaking to you through the following words.**
   • let us fix our eyes on Jesus

   • the author and perfecter of our faith

   • who for the joy set before Him endured the cross

   Are your eyes fixed on Jesus today? Why or why not?

   What does the runner do to get to the finish line?
   • She fixes her mind on the finish line.
   • She concentrates on the path before her.
   • She focuses on running the race.

   Our life is being compared to a race and Jesus is the finish line; therefore, we are to fix our eyes on Jesus. Our mind is to be set on God and His purposes.

5. **Read Psalm 119:34-37. Write out key thoughts.**

Turn your eyes upon Jesus Look full in His wonderful face And the things of earth will grow strangely dim In the light of His glory and grace

∽ Are you focusing on unimportant or worthless things? Explain.

Jesus is the author and perfecter of faith. I find this encouraging because I do not have to perfect faith within myself. The Word says Jesus is the beginning and the end.

6. Write out Philippians 1:6.

Another reason for confidence! The God who loves us, who never changes, will complete His work in us. (There is a reason we keep repeating this verse.)

For the joy set before Him, He endured. That should be our attitude today.

We may not know the outcome of a situation, but we do know that God promises to work in our lives through all things.

You are His gem— Tested, shining and sparkling, You have survived the winds of adversity . . . You are a winner! You are an overcomer! You have credentials! Source Unknown

7. Write out Romans 8:28.

∽ Does it give you joy to know that ALL things are working together in your life? Explain.

∽ Now write out Romans 8:29.

∽ According to this verse, what good is being produced in all things?

∞ What is happening to us through the circumstances and events of life?

∞ Whom were you predestined to be like?

> God loves you just the way you are, but He refuses to leave you there. He wants you to be just like Jesus. Isn't that good news? You aren't stuck with today's personality. You aren't condemned to grumpy-dom. You are changeable. You are tweakable. Even if you've worried each day of your life, you needn't worry the rest of your life. So what if your were born with a sour outlook, you don't have to die with one. God will change you. And He will change you to be just like Jesus. Can you think of a better offer?[2]—*Robert McGee*

∞ Do you have some areas in which you know God wants to work? What are they?

∞ Can you go to God with these areas today? If not, why not?

If we were just like Jesus, we would be women of love. We would see the best, believe the best, and hope in the best. We would also be women of faith. We would know that God is faithful to every one of His promises. Need some changing? I do.

8. Read Hebrews 12:3-5. Read this passage again—out loud. Then journal what God is speaking to you through the following words.
   • consider him . . . so that you will not grow weary and lose heart

- in your struggle . . . you have not yet resisted to the point of shedding blood

- you have forgotten the word of encouragement that addresses you as [daughters]

- my [daughter], do not make light of the Lord's discipline

- do not lose heart when He rebukes you

9. **Write out Hebrews 12:6.**

Read this verse again—out loud. Then journal what God is speaking to you through the following words.

- the Lord disciplines (corrects) those He loves

- He punishes everyone He accepts as a [daughter]

Praise Upon Praise
O Father
Through the years
You have permitted
Hurt upon hurt
In my God-planned life.
This early morning
Even before I greet the dawn
I offer You
Praise upon praise
For You are transforming every hurt
Into a holy hallmark—
A genuine guarantee
Of my permanent identification
With You.
Ruth Harms Calkin [3]

10. **Read Hebrews 12:7-8. Read these verses again—out loud. Then journal what God is speaking to you through the following words.**
   • endure hardship as discipline (correction)

   • God is treating you as [daughters]

   • for what [daughter] is not disciplined by [her] father?

   • if you are not disciplined, then you are illegitimate children

The father/daughter connection may be a hard one for many of you to swallow. Many women did not have good relationships with their fathers. Some women were even abandoned or abused as children. If you are a woman who was hurt in some way by your natural father, that pain goes very deep, and may span many years. That hurt makes it difficult for you to understand this idea of a father who loves.

Maybe you were disciplined, but not out of love. I have talked to women who had the daylights beaten out of them as children. That certainly is not the kind of love/discipline relationship the Bible is referring to here. It might be helpful right now to put everything down and pray that God will begin to make real to you what He is to You as a Father, and how much He loves You.

11. Read Hebrews 12:9-10. Read these verses again—out loud. Then journal what God is speaking to you through the following words.

- we have had human fathers who disciplined us

- how much more should we submit to the Father of our spirits and live!

- our fathers disciplined us . . . as they thought best

- God disciplines us for our good, that we may share in His holiness

It's not enough for Him to own you; He wants to change you. Where you and I might be satisfied with a recliner and refrigerator, He refuses to settle for any dwelling short of a palace. After all, this is His house. No expense is spared. No corners are cut. "Oh the utter extravagance of his work in us who trust him (Ephesians 1:19, TM).

This might explain some of the discomfort in your life. Remodeling of the heart is not always pleasant. We don't object when the Carpenter adds a few shelves, but He's been known to gut the entire west wing. He has such high aspirations for you. God envisions a complete restoration. He won't stop until He is finished. And He won't be finished until we have been shaped "along the . . . lines . . . of his Son (Romans 8:29, TM).[4]
—*Max Lucado*

12. Write out Hebrews 12:11.

Read this verse again—out loud. Then journal what God is speaking to you through the following words.

- no discipline seems pleasant at the time

- but painful

- later on it produces a harvest of righteousness and peace

- for those who have been trained by it

13. Write out Hebrews 12:12-13.

Read these verses again—out loud. Then journal what God is speaking to you through the following words.
- strengthen your feeble arms and weak knees

- make level paths for your feet

- so that the lame may not be disabled, but rather healed

Read Psalm 139:2-4. This psalm also expresses how God is ever present with us, and knows our words, thoughts and deeds.

14. Read Revelation 3:15-19. This is a pretty intense statement of the fact that God knows all, and He may not be pleased with what He knows. Self-sufficient people don't realize their need.

∞ According to Revelation 3:15-19, what will God do to the church of Laodicea as a result of His disappointment with her deeds?

∞ Write out Revelation 3:19.

∞ According to Revelation 3:19 what goes hand in hand with God's love?

∞ What does God tell us to do because of this?

15. Read Revelation 3:20. God stands at the door of your heart today. Do you need to repent of something? (Repenting is turning away from something, going in another direction.) What is it?

We often think of repenting in terms of "BIG" sins. But, God tells us we need to be in tune with any of our attitudes and actions that are not pleasing to God. They may not be big things to others, but if He is convicting your heart, then you need to repent and turn away from that attitude or action.

∞ Read Jeremiah 18:1-6.

We are all being shaped by the discipline of our heavenly Father. He shapes and molds us as a potter does clay on a potter's wheel. Being reshaped is sometimes uncomfortable, but the end result is a masterpiece.

God shapes our lives as it seems best to Him. Often His ways make no sense to us, but we must remember that He is God, and we are not. Part of the problem with the new age philosophy is that people are focusing all their energy on shaping themselves into something important and worthwhile. The Bible says in Psalm 127:1, unless the Lords shapes us, it is in vain. You and I do not know what shape our lives are meant to take, but the God who created us knows full well. I would much rather trust my life to the one who is the author of it, the creator of it, than to anyone or anything else.

If the Lord delights in a [woman's] way,
he makes [her] steps firm;

though [she] stumble, [she] will not fall,
for the Lord upholds [her] with his hand
(Psalm 37:23).

Dear Lord,

There are so many things in me that need Your touch. Help me to trust You when Your touch has to be less than gentle. I realize that You are working in me and using my circumstances to make me more like You . . . and I thank You for that. Just help me to keep my focus on You and Your purposes. Lord, I do want to be more like You. In fact, I do want to be just like You. I submit to the work of Your Spirit and ask You to do Your grand and glorious work in my life. Amen.

Love Changes Me

"For I am confident that He who began a good work will carry it out to completion"(Phil. 1:6).

Most of us want to change. Proof of that is the varied menu of growth and self- improvement courses offered in churches, colleges, and community groups. Part of the reason we desire change is because, whether we realize it or not, we desire growth. When we are growing, our lives are moving forward and we experience direction and fulfillment.

One of the synonyms of change is *transform*. In our study, we have been paying close attention to the word *transformation*. As Romans 12:2 says, we are not to be conformed to this world, but TRANSFORMED by the renewing of our minds. We can conclude then, that we will be changed as we grow in our relationship with God. Do you want or need change today?

> God loves to decorate. God has to decorate. Let him live long enough in a heart, and that heart will begin to change. Portraits of hurt will be replaced by landscapes of grace. Walls of anger will be demolished and shaky foundations restored. God can no more leave a life unchanged than a mother can leave her child's tear untouched.[1] —*Max Lucado*

1. Look up *change* in the dictionary. Write the definition here.

There are two definitions of change that I found meaningful: to make different; to exchange.

I am so grateful that by the power of the Holy Spirit I can change and I can be different. There are things within me that need to be uprooted by the Lord if my life is going to grow and bear fruit. I love the idea of *exchange* because God exchanged His life that I might have an abundant and full life. He also will exchange His nature for my selfish nature when I ask Him to do so. My part is coming to Him, with "me."

> How easy it is to fall into the trap of making a bold profession of a vital spiritual life when our number-one priority is seeking to please the flesh! Certainly the power that our fallen nature can hold over us is one of the biggest problems we face in life. How can we be free from the seemingly unconquerable bondage to the flesh?
>
> The simple yet profound answer is this: Don't fight the flesh, strengthen the Spirit! Don't fight against the darkness; turn on the light.[2]—*Chuck Smith*

2. Write out Hebrews 4:16.

∽ One of our studies dealt with confidence. Here in this verse you are instructed to approach God with confidence. What do you think that means?

As we begin to grow and change in our understanding of God's love, we will feel more comfortable going to God with all our weaknesses and inse-curities. It is when we go to Him that we find grace to help us in our everyday needs. The grace of God will do for us that which we could never do for ourselves. That is the exchanged life!

Every day we have choices to make. Sometimes we make wise choices, and sometimes we make questionable choices. In either case, we all have things in our lives that cause us a great amount of anxiety and that can be changed. We all obsess at times over things that are not changeable, and we need to learn to accept those things that we cannot change.

In order to release some of these target areas to God, it will be helpful for you to take a personal inventory.

- Make a list of all the things you do not like about yourself or your life. Be specific.

- Now go through that list and put a check by all the things that cannot be changed. These things will need to be committed to God. They cannot be changed; you must learn to trust God with them and accept them.

- Make a second list that includes everything from the first list that does not have a check. These are the things that can be changed. This is your new target list. This list should become a focus in your prayers.

Now spend some time praying about the inventory you just finished.

First, give God all the things that cannot be changed. You must accept these things because they cannot change. No amount of self-pity will change them, but your acceptance of them will give you a new attitude about them. Give them and your attitude to God, and ask Him to give you the grace to accept the things you cannot change.

Next, take the new list and look it over closely. You may have several things on your list that can actually change—such as disorganization, procrastination, hair style, weight, etc. (For most women much of this list revolves around appearances or performance. Sadly, we spend so much energy looking at the outside, don't we?) With this new list in hand, the first thing you need to do is admit the fact that though you have tried changing some of these areas in the past, you have been unsuccessful. This time you need to start by asking God for His power to work in you in all these areas. You need to concentrate on drawing close to Him, turning on the light in areas that have been dark! Your spirit needs to be fed, filled, and strengthened.

Some things may have been dragging you down for years, and the distraction of never dealing with them has caused more anxiety than they're worth. It seems common for us to think that we have to live with all of our bad habits and basic "yuk." Evidently, some of us have bought into a idea that if God wants it changed, He will just change it. But, we have choices regarding the changeable things that keep us down. Every day God allows us to make choices. The most important choice of each day is walking in the Spirit.

> When we walk in the Spirit, living in constant awareness of the presence of God, we no longer need others to nag and preach at us about living up to Christian standards. Our lives will be revolutionized as we keep the nearness and love of God in the front of our minds.[3] —*Chuck Smith*

Our personal areas of struggle can continue to keep us self-focused, or we can ask God for His wisdom and strength in dealing with the particular problem. Choose today to make the wisest choice—surrendering to God for His help and strength.

Proverbs 3:6 says, "In all your ways acknowledge him, and *he will make your paths straight*" (italics added). Could this mean that in Him you can find the direction you need to help you with your weaknesses and change your life? You bet!

> God grant me the serenity
> to accept the things I cannot change
> the courage to change the things I can
> And, the wisdom to know the difference.[4] —*Reinhold Niebuhr*

3. Write out John 16:33.

∞ What does John 16:33 say you will have in this life?

∞ What attitude does this verse say you should have toward a less than perfect life?

∞ Why are you to have cheer?

> Look at this definition of *cheer* from Webster's:
>   good spirits;
>   something providing happiness or joy;
>   encouragement;
>   to fill with happiness.

With the above definitions in mind, think of what it might mean to be of good cheer. You can be filled with happiness and joy and be encouraged in your spirit because He has overcome the world, and all of those unchangeable challenges that we face.

The Greek word in this passage is *tharseo,* which means to have courage.

I am to face life with courage. Though life can be difficult, my inner strength and courage come from knowing Jesus, and trusting that He is working in and through all things that touch my individual life.

Sometimes I throw my own pity party. Instead of balloons and cupcakes, I have Kleenex and tears—all because I cannot get a handle on a particular situation, and I just want it fixed today. The pity party approach is in contrast to the "cheer" approach I see here in God's Word. The pity party isn't a celebration of courage but rather a statement of discouragement. I need to climb out of the pit of pity as quickly as I can. It is a trap that leads to the exact opposite of cheer. Part of God's changing me is a radical change in perspective as a result of a different life focus and the empowering of God's Holy Spirit.

Satan's first attack upon the human race was his sly effort to destroy Eve's confidence in the kindness of God. From that day, men have had a false conception of God. Nothing twists and deforms the soul more than a low or unworthy conception of God. The God of the Pharisees was not a God easy to live with.

From a failure to properly understand God comes a world of unhappiness among good Christians even today. The Christian life is thought to be a glum, unrelieved cross-carrying under the eye of a stern Father who expects much and excuses nothing.

> The truth is that God is the most winsome of all beings and His service one of unspeakable pleasure. He loves us for ourselves and values our love more than galaxies of new created worlds.[5]—*A. W. Tozer*

We do not need to be throwing pity parties. Ladies, God loves us, and He is in control!! Change those negative tapes . . . replace them with the truth.

4. **Read Philippians 4:4-13. These verses give some instructions for accepting life's circumstances.**

∽ Write out the instructions you see, and then write the promises of this text in the space below:

LESSONS/INSTRUCTIONS TO ME	PROMISES/CHANGES IN ME
Example: Rejoice	Example: I will have peace

5. Write out Philippians 4:19.

∞ Is this a promise you can stand on? Do you suspect that God's Word can change your mind and change your life? Why or why not?

6. Read John 16:33 again. Do you think that in this verse Jesus was warning His disciples life would be difficult? Why was He doing this?

In this world you will have tribulation. This is reality.
Troubles
Affliction
Distress

∞ In John 16:33 how did Jesus point the disciples in a positive direction in terms of accepting a difficult life?

7. Write out 1 Peter 5:10.

∞ Instead of promising you that He will change all the circumstances of your life, what does God promise you, according to 1 Peter 5:10?

God's Word says He will make you strong, firm, and steadfast after you have suffered awhile. It is clear that the hard times in our lives can be tools to shape us into greater strength; these things can be used to change us.

Once we have come to accept that some of the situations, people, or things in our lives cannot be changed, we learn to be content. It's like exhaling . . . letting out all that steam that kept us bound in frustration before.

Now we will look at trusting God in the things that can be changed.

8. Read John chapter 14. Write out verse 16. Remember that the Holy Spirit is your source for change.

As we have previously studied, the Holy Spirit is called our helper. The same Holy Spirit that Jesus was talking about here in the book of John indwells each believer. It is awesome to think that I have within me the Holy Spirit of God.

Often we forget that God's Spirit has been given to us. Scripture tells us we weren't left as orphans, but we have received the Spirit of God. Recently, I have made it a practice to remind myself every day that the Holy Spirit indwells me. It's an exciting adventure to watch the Holy Spirit work through me in the daily things of life.

> In great simplicity and restfulness believe in Him as having given His own Spirit within you. Accept this as the secret of the life of Christ in you: the Holy Spirit is dwelling in the hidden recesses of your spirit. Meditate on it, believe Jesus and His word concerning it, until your soul bows with holy fear and awe before God under the glory of the truth: the Holy Spirit of God is, indeed, dwelling in me.
>
> Yield yourself to His leading. We have seen that leading is not just in the mind or thoughts, but in the life and disposition. Yield yourself to God, to be guided by the Holy Spirit in all your conduct.[6]—*Andrew Murray*

In this new age era, it is not uncommon to hear that we need to ask "a spirit to guide us," or that we should "pray to the light." What spirit, and what light? The light of yourself? The spirit of the universe? Sadly, in the rush to find our purpose and dip into some spirituality, many of us are paying big bucks to get in touch with ourselves and/or some spiritual guide.

How wonderful that as Christians we need to search no more! Jesus Christ is the light, and He gave us His Spirit to be our guide. Best of all, we don't have to pay big bucks for what God has freely given. In John 14:6 Jesus said, "I am the way and the truth and the life."

I am excited to live in-tune to the Holy Spirit of God, relying on the power of the Holy Spirit to give me the strength I need in all areas of life. Unfortunately, like everyone else, I forget to rely on the Holy Spirit as much as I should. I let areas go unchecked and unchanged because they just seem so overwhelming and hard for me to change and because I forget that through Christ all things are possible. I keep trying on my own, and end up running out of steam. *Hello? Is anyone there? Where am I to go for help?*

Today I challenge you to begin to rely on the Holy Sprit of God for every area of change that showed up on your inventory list earlier in this lesson. As I challenge you, I also challenge myself. For it is time that we take hold of what Christ has promised us and live in the fullness of His strength and the fullness of His Spirit's power.

9. Write out John 16:13-14.

Change is the byproduct of growth.

G	God
R	Restoring
O	Our
W	Whole Life
T	Through
H	His Son Jesus

Growth does not happen overnight; it happens in small increments over a period of time. I like to think of it as baby steps. But, growth is not possible unless the conditions are right. Just as a garden is grown with proper nurturing and care, so the growth in our lives is produced with the proper attachment to the Vine. We do not make the fruit appear, for we cannot produce it in and of ourselves. Our part is staying attached to the source of life and power that can produce beautiful and lasting fruit.

These days you can send messages across the world at the speed of light. You can cross the Atlantic in under three hours. You can microwave a whole meal in minutes. You can even get your dry cleaning back the same day! We move in a fast-paced society where everything is now. We don't want to wait. We ask for it and it's there.

Sometimes we try to carry over that attitude to our relationship with God. We wonder, What are the shortcuts? What are the easy angles? What's the inside track? I'm sorry, but there aren't any shortcuts, there are no easy angles. The only way to spiritual growth is to abide. Sink your roots deeply into Jesus Christ and continually walk with Him, and in time you will see fruit.[7] —*Greg Laurie*

10. Read John 15. Write out verse 5.

∞ What does John 15 tell you happens in your life when you abide in Christ?

∞ What happens when you are apart from Him?

Abiding in Christ is having a relationship With Him. Remember the three R's from the beginning of the study?

REMAIN

RENEW

REST

The very first "R" is Remain, and it is the most important one. To Remain in Christ is to abide in Him, or to be connected to Him. I like to think of myself as daily connecting to the power source of life. When I think of it that way, I get a surge of excitement and anticipation each morning. It is living a God-dependent life.

When I am tempted with the thoughts: *you can't do that, you don't have enough skill, it is too hard for you . . . etc.,* I am able to say, "All things are possible for those who abide in Christ." I am so empowered in the strength of God as I make that statement, and add to it, "apart from Him I am nothing." These words have become my motto. They empower me because they remind me to stay close, connected, and attached to Him. They remind me daily to REMAIN, and then I am RENEWED, and as a result I can REST. My life is then in the growth phase, on the road to restoration, and things do begin to change!

You may be thinking, *I am nothing?* Well, I do plenty of things, and I don't think it is Christ who is doing all of them. It is me.

John 15 says we can do nothing that will honor Christ and bring life-changing restorative power apart from Christ and His Spirit. Yes, you have abilities, but think of the power in which those natural abilities can be used when you ask the Holy Spirit to do those things through you. It's exciting! It's like turning up the voltage. When we abide in Christ, we are using our gifts and abilities for His purposes, empowered by a source much bigger, wiser, and mightier than ourselves.

11. Write out Galatians 5:22-23.

This fruit is the very nature of the Holy Spirit. It is important that we learn it, and not just in our heads. This fruit can be a key in giving us the power to walk in the Spirit.

Let's suppose that one of the areas of change you are praying about is your harshness. The Bible tells us here that the fruit of the Spirit is gentleness and kindness. So you can boldly and confidently ask the Holy Spirit of God to work within you, filling you with the strength and power of God. Your prayer should be for the exchange to happen. That is, that He would exchange the harshness for gentleness and kindness by His Spirit working within you, and by His Spirit convicting you and leading you on the pathway to change.

12. Read Psalm 18. Circle or underline all the times that David refers to strength. (This psalm was written while David was in battle. Likewise, when you are trying to conquer old, bad, and ingrained habits you are in battle! Just as the Lord was David's source of strength, so He can be yours today.)

∞ Write out Psalm 68:19.

∞ According to this verse, who daily bears your burdens?

∞ Journal your thoughts here about the message in this psalm as it relates to you today and the areas that you are committing to God for change.

13. Write out the following verses:

∞ Psalm 29:11.

∞ Psalm 84: 5.

∞ Psalm 105:4.

It is important to remember that you cannot change everything all at once. We tend to want to fix things immediately. Even the things that can be changed need to be taken one by one to the Lord for His direction and strength. He can give us plans for change because He knows the entire situation better than anyone else. If there are deep-rooted problems lurking that are preventing change, guess who knows? He gives us a plan by directing us to His Word and by bringing light to areas that were formerly dark or confused.

In this lesson, you compiled a list of changeable things. It is my suggestion that you take from that list the thing that drags you down the most and start there. Make that one area your point of prayer today. *Caution:* Don't try to change yourself in your own power and strength. Just trust that God, by His grace, will give you what you need to change one area at a time. He will meet you in the most exciting and practical ways.

Remember : " 'not by might nor by power, but by my Spirit' says the Lord" (Zechariah 4:6).

We must trust in the God who never changes!

14. **Write out Malachi 3:6 and Hebrews 13:8. Underline the key words in each verse.**

May the God of all peace give you His strength as you trust Him for change in your life!

> Now the Lord is the Spirit, and where the Spirit of the Lord is, there is freedom. And we, who with unveiled faces all reflect the Lord's glory, are being transformed into his likeness, with ever increasing glory, which comes from the Lord, who is the Spirit (2 Corinthians 3:17-18).

It is my prayer that we all will have unveiled faces before the Lord, holding nothing back from the God who knows us better than we know ourselves.

Memorize the verse that spoke to you most significantly this week. Write it on an index card. Personalize it and make it your own! Share with someone the areas that you need God's strength to change and have that person pray for you.

Remember: take the one most significant area and begin praying for God's plan of action, then be obedient to His leading.

Don't Stop Lord
Lord
In asking You
To make me whole
I certainly didn't know
What I was in for.
You have ransacked me
Until I sometimes feel
There is nothing left.
But don't stop, Lord
Please don't stop!
I'm trusting that the product
Will be worth the process.
Ruth Harms Calkin [8]

Dear Lord,

Too often I look at others around me and calculate all the changes that they need in their lives. I don't want to do that anymore. Instead, I want to busy myself looking at my own life and my own heart, actions, and attitudes. I ask You to change me from the inside out. Turn my world upside down if You need to so that my heart can be turned right side up! I am Yours. Fill me anew with Your precious Spirit and give me the strength and grace to walk in the power of your Spirit each and every day, instead of in my own feeble strength. Amen.

LOVE GIVES ME HOPE

"Let us hold unswervingly to the hope we profess for He who promised is faithful"(Heb. 10:23).

The world we live in today is full of challenges. It is not the "Leave It to Beaver" of the '50s and '60s. We live in a world littered with broken families, shattered dreams, addictions, promiscuity, crime, etc. Jesus knew that the world would be a hard place to live in. That is why He gave us so many directives in advance. It is amazing how relevant the Bible is today, even though it was written so long ago.

In this lesson we are going to concentrate on hope. We will look at what it means to have hope, how to have hope, and how to battle today's hope-lessness. The love of God will never leave us or forsake us. He is a constant anchor in this sea of life, and that means that in the midst of the storms we can learn to have hope!

1. Read Psalm 146. (If possible, read this psalm out loud.) Then underline the verses that are speaking to your heart and write your thoughts about them.

∞ What does Psalm 146:3 tell you not to do?

∞ Have you put your trust in mortal men (husband, friends, children, relatives)? Why?

Too often we base everything on what people think of us. We put our trust in their belief system, and in their love, rather than in God's love.

> We do not have to be successful or have to be pleasing to others to have a healthy sense of self-esteem and worth. That worth has freely and conclusively been given to us by God. Failure and/or the disapproval of others can't take it away![1]
> —Robert McGee

∞ Who is blessed according to Psalm 146:5?

∞ What are some of the descriptions of the Lord in Psalm 146:5-6?

2. Psalm 146:7-10 paints what kind of picture of God's character?

Hope: to want or wish for with a feeling of confident expectation

Hopeless: to have no confident expectation

∞ Is this a God in whom you can have hope? Why or why not?

David began this psalm and ended it with praise to God because He is a God who is so incredibly faithful that we can put all our hope in Him.

∞ Are you in the middle of a hopeless situation? What is it?

Sometimes our circumstances make it hard to have expectations and confidence. Yet, we can live in confidence when we are not moved by the circumstances around us, but instead encouraged and stilled by our hope in God. We need to understand that God has plans for us. . . . Yes, He does!

∞ Write out Jeremiah 29:11.

3. Read Hebrews 11:1-6. What are the key words or thoughts here?

4. Write out Hebrews 10:23.

∞ Write out Hebrews 10:35. Remember: do not throw away your hope.

5. Read Hebrews 13:5-6. What won't God ever do to you?

∞ What adjective is used in Hebrews 13:5-6 to describe God?

6. Write out the following verses:

∞ Psalm 147:11.

∞ Proverbs 13:12.

7. Look up *deferred* in the dictionary. Write the definition here.

∞ Look up Proverbs 13:12 in another translation if possible. Can you relate to deferred hope?

8. Write out Isaiah 40:31.

∞ What are the key words in Isaiah 40:31?

∞ What does Isaiah 40:31 mean to you?

∞ This verse suggests that hope in God will give you a direction and a promise. What are they?

9. Read Romans 5:1-5. What do you have with God?

∞ According to Romans 5:1-5, where do you stand with God?

∞ In what do you rejoice?

⌒ What does character produce?

⌒ What will hope not do?

All of us know about trials, sufferings, and the things that produce character. I have experienced so much over the past ten years, that I should be a *real character* by now! Many of you probably feel the same way. We tire of life's problems, partly because they are just plain hard and tire us out, and partly because we need a new perspective on what good can come out of the hard stuff. But God's Word tells us to rejoice in our sufferings! Rejoice? How can we do that? Are we crazy? In denial?

NO! On the contrary, we are being lead into truth by the Spirit of God, who teaches us the things of God. And, one of those great things of God is that He is able to take the ugliness of our lives and produce good things in us. After we have gone through it awhile, we develop more character, and then character gives birth to HOPE—confident expectation. We can have confident expectation because of the unfailing love of God that never changes.

One of the definitions of character is: a certain disposition. I like this definition because as I persevere, God develops in me a certain disposition of confidence in Him. As I learn of God's love for me, I develop a disposition of trust, security, and confidence. All my hope is in God.

Faith and hope go hand in hand.

Faith is the belief that God is real and that God is good. Faith is not a mystical experience or a midnight vision or a voice in the forest. . . . It is a choice to believe that the one who made it all hasn't left it all and that He still sends light into the shadows and responds to gestures of faith. . . .

Faith is not the belief that God will do what you want. Faith is the belief that God will do what is right. God's economy is upside down (or rightside up and ours is upside down!).

> God says that the more hopeless your circumstances, the more likely your salvation. The greater your cares, the more genuine your prayers. The darker the room, the greater the need for light.[2] —*Max Lucado*

10. Write out Romans 12:12. This verse tells you to do three things. List them.

∞ What does "be joyful in hope" mean to you?

I once knew a woman who seemed to skip through life. She had her share of challenges—breast cancer, and divorce after twenty-seven years, to name a few. Yet, through her pain and heartache, she continued to smile and place her hope in God. She reminded me of someone skipping through a field of flowers without a care in the world. At first I thought she was just in some *big denial* of her life's situation. Then I got to know her better.

I found that she was a woman who had a relationship with God in a very real and practical way. Her relationship with Him had been tried and tested through some of the cruelest storms, yet she never gave up. She was faithful in prayer. She prayed about all her needs every day. This was her method of survival, and it brought her great peace of mind and joy.

Too many times, people look at Christians and think they would never want to be like us . . . we worry more than they do! Unfortunately, it is true that we live like hopeless people much of the time. This is a sad statement of fact. Something should be different in a Christian's life, don't you think? And, I'm not talking about having it all together, because we are not perfect and never will be. But something in our disposition should point to the hope we have in God.

We should be living in the confidence that He loves us, that His very nature is love, and that His nature is fixed, firm, and unchanging! Because of this unchanging nature of God, we can rest in the facts of His faithfulness.

∞ On what is your hope fixed in today? Why?

11. Write out Romans 15:4.

Scripture is meant to encourage us! It is intended to be a positive, not a negative. The world we live in makes it a negative with the attitude of, "Those Christians can't do anything. They have so many rules. They are no fun!"

When actually, the positive truth is: God came to give us a full life in Him. We can have plenty of fun, plenty of joy, and plenty of peace. But, we must have the encouragement of the Scriptures to teach us.

This week, memorize the verse that meant the most to you. Share your hope with others!

12. In closing this week's lesson, look up Colossians 1:27-29 and rewrite it in your own words.

The most wonderful thing we have to hope in is the fact that Christ is in us. He dwells within us even though we are ordinary women. He is the hope that this life isn't the final call for us. And, it is His energy that works in and through us with power. This is awesome. Do you ever take for granted the fact that Christ is in you? I know that I do, but when I slow down, exhale, take a breath, and let it sink in amazing things happen. I am not only filled with hope, but also with joy, and definitely with CONFIDENCE in Christ!

Our faith in God should make a difference in our daily lives. It should not be reduced to a Sunday School faith that only is brought out for church.

We have this hope as an anchor for the soul, firm and secure (Hebrews 6:19).

We can proclaim to our unsaved friends and neighbors that we have a relationship with the Living God, and that is why we are growing in hope and confidence. We are growing in the knowledge of His great love for us, and that gives us a new attitude! Nothing is impossible when we have faith in God, and when we hope in Him.

It is My will that your entire person expresses praises to My Name,
It is My will that you count your body as precious,
that you do not compare yourself to others,
nor be threatened by years or infirmities,
but that your mind be solidly fixed on Me,
whole and full of My salvation.
You are not a partial person
not even if you believe it to be true.
Marie Chapian [3]

Dear Lord,

When I think about Your love, I am filled with hope. My heart is full and my mind at ease when the bigness of Your love is my focal point. If instead, I stop and look at myself or at others as a basis for happiness and security, I fall flat on my face. I must be reminded over and over again that You are my hope. You are the One in whom I will put my hope and trust. O, precious Father, by the power of Your Spirit fill me with the hope of heaven and the truth of eternity. May this hope keep me steady while I walk in the paths You have given me to tread while here on earth. Amen.

LOVE HAS NO FEAR

"I will protect him, for he acknowledges my name"(Psalm 91:14).

Have you ever been struck by fear? Have you ever been stopped dead in your tracks by the kind of fear that is heart-wrenching, stomach-achy, head-throbbing, and all encompassing? What about anxiety? It is another form of fear, worrying relentlessly over the details of the future, or obsessing over the outcome of any given situation. Have you known anxiety? When I am anxious for any length of time, it seems as though my body goes down with me. Fear is awful!

There are many variations and levels of fear and anxiety. Unfortunately, I have mastered them all. I was a child who was unusually fearful. As I grew up, my fears only magnified, while the veneer I wore to hide the fears thickened. By the time I was in fifth grade, I was diagnosed with ulcers. Though my fears seemed unusual to me, and though I wanted out of them, I could not get over the hurdle of fear.

The evening I accepted Christ was the first glimpse I had that my fears could be conquered. For that moment in time, all fears were gone. The things I obsessed over and dreaded became so faded in the distance that I barely recognized them anymore. I felt free for the first time in almost eighteen years.

I wish I could tell you that my freedom from fear lasted indefinitely, and that fear, worry, and anxiety never raised their ugly heads again. But, that is not the truth. I can say with confidence that as I grow in my relationship with Jesus, the story of fear in my life is playing out with a happy ending.

As I grow in relationship with the Father, my fears decrease. And, as I understand the love of God toward me, fear, worry, and anxiety are much less frequent guests in my mind and in my body. My glimpse of freedom upon salvation was a glimpse of what was to come as I grew to know the love of God for me. It is in understanding His love and seeking Him that I am delivered from the bondage of fear and worry. It is His love that fills me with confidence and trust in the God who protects me and watches over me with loving care.

1. **Read Psalm 139:5-10. (I know you keep reading Psalm 139, but bear with me. You will be glad you did. Pay close attention to these words as if you have never read them before.)**

∞ What are these verses saying to you in regard to protection?

∞ Draw a square box. Write your name in the center of the box.

∞ How does this box illustrate Psalm 139:5?

In Psalm 139:5 I find relief. Just to think that God goes before me, follows behind me, and places His Hand on me gives me a picture of God enclosing me in His love. David even says in verse 6 that this is a fact too wonderful to understand fully. He goes on to describe how God is always with him, and then he ends this thought beautifully in verse 10, when he says, "your hand will guide me, your right hand will hold me fast."

It is very important for us to understand that God does protect us and that He does hold us in His hand.

2. **Write out the following verses:**

∞ Psalm 31:15.

∞ Psalm 37:24.

∞ John 10:28-29.

∞ According to the verses above, where do you reside today?

You cannot see the hands of God, but it is essential to believe by faith that they are there upholding you, protecting you, and guiding you.

3. Write out 1 John 4:18.

∞ What are the key words in 1 John 4:18?

Instead of experiencing "NO FEAR," many of us "Know Fear" and struggle to understand why we just cannot get a grip on our fears.

∞ Make a list of the things that you are most fearful of today.

Fear:
alarm or agitation
caused by expecta-
tion or realization
of danger;
dread or appre-
hension;
to be frightened or
worried;
to be timid;
panic or terror.

∞ Do you think God is big enough to take care of the things on your list that are holding you in the grip of fear? Why or why not?

> Two little girls were talking about God, and one said, "I know God does not love me. He could not care for such a tiny little girl like me."
>
> "Dear me, Sis." said the other girl, "don't you know that is just what God is for—to take care of tiny little girls who can't take care of themselves, just like us."
>
> "Is He?" said the first little girl, "I did not know that. Then I don't need to worry anymore, do I?[1]—*Hannah Whitall Smith*

4. **What are some of the characteristics of God's love that you have learned during the other lessons in this study, that could help you understand why 1 John 4:18 says, "There is no fear in love"? (Refer to the definition of Love in 1 Corinthians 13.)**

∞ Why do you think love drives out fear?

First John 4:18 says, "The one who fears is not made perfect in love." This actually means that we have not matured in love while fear is present in us. It is a personal prayer of mine to understand the love of God in such a way that fear would not be present in me. I realize that there are times of "normal" fear, such as the apprehension when you see someone coming straight for your bumper through the rearview mirror, or when you walk into your house after a burglary. We will all experience a moment of fear now and then. This is normal. It is these kinds of fears that cause us to wear seat belts and lock our doors. These fears act as the guidelines for common sense.

The fear this verse talks about is the fear that torments and punishes you. The fear that things are not going to be OK with you. The kind of fear that says, "There is not a God of love watching over me." It is the kind of fear that has reduced God's love and protection to some a fairy tale instead of the very real strength and power that it is.

> There is no fear in love—dread does not exist; but full-grown (complete, perfect) love turns fear out of doors and expels every trace of terror! For fear brings with it the thought of punishment, and [so] he who is afraid has not reached the full maturity of love—is not yet grown into love's complete perfection (1 John 4:18, AMP).

5. **All the fears you listed are your cares—those things that concern you. Write out 1 Peter 5:7.**

∞ What does 1 Peter 5:7 instruct you to do with your fears, concerns, and cares?

Do you know how to cast your cares upon the Lord? If you do not understand this concept, it is very basic. Cast means: to throw, to fling, to shed, to turn over. To cast your cares upon the Lord means you turn your worries and fears over to Him. You throw them all on His shoulders. This requires communication, which is prayer. Tell God everything—pour out your heart to Him. You can do this in a quiet place, or you can do it driving down the freeway. Hey, if people can negotiate business deals over a cellular phone on the freeway, you surely can negotiate handing your life's circumstances over to God while you are driving! You don't even need a cellular phone. Just dial 333 (Jeremiah 33:3)!

∞ Write out how you go about (or will go about) casting your cares upon the Lord.

6. Write out Jeremiah 33:3.

   One of the greatest things we do not fully understand is God's love and concern for us. As we call out to Him, He will make us sure in His love!

7. Read Psalm 34:4-7. What does this passage say you are to do?

∽ According to these verses, what is the consequence of seeking God?

∽ How is your countenance affected by seeking God?

∽ According to Psalm 34:4-7, where is the angel of the Lord?

8. Read Psalm 91. What is the main theme of this psalm?

∽ According to this psalm, where are you supposed to dwell?

∽ What does God command the angels to do for you?

∽ Read this psalm again—out loud. Let the meaning sink into your heart!

9. Read Psalm 23. If you think of this as a funeral text, ask the Holy Spirit to clear your mind and speak the truth of this psalm to you personally in a new way. What does David say he will not fear?

Often we fear the worst. We seem to think the good things are reserved for someone else who deserves them, and we will just have to struggle through the hard knocks, or the "worst" of life. This pattern of thinking is contrary to the Word of God, isn't it? Psalm 23:6 says, "Surely goodness and love will follow me all the days of my life." These words were not written by someone fearing the worst! We cannot say, "I will fear no evil," unless we have an understanding of "goodness and love" following us all the days of our life.

Stop now and pray that God will make it real to you that He is your Shepherd. A shepherd is someone who takes care of the sheep. He feeds them, exercises them, protects them, and pulls them back in when they've gone astray. God is your shepherd.

David understood that God was his shepherd and what that meant. Therefore he was able to say, " I will fear no evil." Oh, that we may know God and His love in this same way, so that we too can confidently say, "goodness and love follow me."

10. Read Romans 8:15 and Romans 8:28-39. What is the key thought in these passages?

℃ What are the key words in these passages?

I find two thoughts incredibly encouraging:
- all things work together for my good;
- nothing can separate me from the love of God.

I have gone through many things, and when I see that no "thing" can separate me from the love of God and that every "thing" will work together for my eventual good and growth, I am released from the need to worry or fear. But I must remind myself of these truths, and that cannot be accomplished in a one-shot glance at Scripture that makes me feel warm and fuzzy. I must have firmly planted within me the truth that I have no need to fear because God

is my shepherd;

is for me;

is with me;
works in my circumstances for good;
cannot be separated from me;
gives His angels command to protect me;
delivers me from evil.

Tell yourself the truth today . . . think God's thoughts!

In Romans 8:15 do you get the idea that the reason we are not slaves any longer to sin is because we have a "Father" relationship going with the Lord? Romans 8:17 calls us to remember we are His children.

11. What are your thoughts about Romans 8:15 and Romans 8:17?

12. Read Matthew 7:9-11. What is the key thought here?

Do you think that sometimes you worry just because you expect the worst, the "evil," to happen to you? These verses in Matthew say that we are His children, and He desires to give us good things! Remember to cast your cares on Him, seek Him, and ask Him (pray).

13. Read Matthew 8:23-27. How does this relate to you today?

Isn't it true that we have such little faith? We are tossed all about, even though the Lord has always had our lives under control. We may not like some of our circumstances, but remember . . . we live in an imperfect world. God never promised to deliver us from the hardships of life, but rather in the midst of those hardships He has promised to deliver us from the fear, anxiety, and torment as we put our faith in Him.

Do you need Jesus to calm a storm in your life today? Pray, and ask Him to do just what He did in Matthew 8.

Remember, He loves to give His children good gifts. His power at work in us is one of His good gifts!

14. Read Matthew 10:28-31. Of what are you not to be afraid?

∞ According to these verses, what is one of the things God knows about you?

∞ What does this passage say about your worth or value?

Fear Not

Again and again, dear Lord
I read Your words, "Fear not."
Surely You would not say it so often
If there were any reason to fear.
Nor would You command it so explicitly
If You could not keep me from fearing.
God, You have given me a Fear Not
For every puzzling circumstance
For every possible emergency
For every trial and testing
Real or imagined.
Yet I confess wasted hours—
Even days, dear Lord
When fear clutches and clobbers me
Until I am physically and emotionally spent.
Lord, when David cried to You
You delivered him from all his fears.
On this gray-sky morning

> I kneel before You with David's cry.
> O my Father, I cannot believe
> You would be less kind to me
> Than You were to David.
> *Ruth Harms Calkin* [2]

15. Read Matthew 6:25-34. (This is a repeat for a reason . . . check it out!) After reading these verses, sum up this entire lesson and the reason you do not need to fear.

⌒ According to Matthew 6:25-34, how are you supposed to live?

So do not fear, for I am with you; do not be dismayed, for I am your God. I will strengthen you and help you; I will uphold you with my righteous right hand (Isaiah 41:10).

Remember: fear is the opposite of faith.

Dear Lord,

Forgive me for trusting in alarm systems and security devices more than I trust in You. I have let fears consume me at times. Father, teach me Your love in such a deep and profound way that I have no need of fear in my life. I desire to know You in a life-changing way. I thank You that You always keep me in Your grasp and that nothing can separate me from Your love. I want to please You and live by faith, instead of fear. Amen

*L*OVE LIFTS ME TO NEW HEIGHTS

"Because your love is better than life, my lips will glorify you. I will praise you as long as I live" (Psalm 63:3–4).

Several years ago there was a popular song, "Up Where We Belong."

> Love lift us up where we belong
> where the eagles fly, on a mountain high
> Love lifts us up where we belong
> far from the world we know
> where cool breezes blow . . .[1]

We want to be lifted up above the gunk of life, not because we want to escape it entirely, but because we know that our faith in Christ should be real enough to lift us above our circumstances into the land of faith, hope, love, and trust.

Unfortunately, not many of us are living consistently up where we belong. Don't get me wrong, this lesson is not about following man-made rules and regulations. On the contrary, this lesson is about following God right up to the place that He has designed for us to live—the land of faith, hope, and understanding His love.

When you are secure in a love relationship, you act securely. You do things that secure people do. You accept, love, honor, and trust that the other partner in the relationship is doing the same. The level of trust and security breathes a new kind of life into the relationship. On the other end of the spectrum, when a relationship is not getting proper attention, those involved in the relationship experience insecurity and fears. They behave in a way that is contrary to love, but is instead, selfish, immature, and self-seeking. The lack of security in this kind of relationship discourages a bond with the other person, and instead encourages separation and disillusionment.

In our relationship with Christ, we must acknowledge that we are in a secure relationship. His Word says that nothing can separate us from the love of God, and no one can pluck us from our Father's hand. In this relationship it would be fitting for us to accept His Word, love Him with every part of us, and honor Him by trusting Him with all of our heart. This kind of interaction on our part breeds in us the type of love relationship with our maker that promotes trust and security and instills confidence. It lifts us to a better place. It causes us to stretch to new heights in Him.

Now is the time to walk in that love relationship that God has already provided for us. It is time for His love to lift us up where we belong.

1. Read Colossians 2:20-22 and Colossians 3:1-3. Then rewrite these passages, including the theme of each one, in your own words. Personalize them in a way that can be applied to your life.

2. According to Colossians 3:1, on what are you to set your heart and mind?

∞ Do you find this is a struggle? Why or why not?

3. Write out the following verses:

∽ Isaiah 48:17.

∽ Proverbs 3:5-7.

Just how important is it to seek God on a daily basis? It is crucial! There is no way to have our minds set on things above if we are not in relationship with God. There is no way your marriage, or any relationship, will grow without attention and quality time. The more time spent, the more attention given the relationship, the more it grows. Time spent with the Lord is like fertilizer to our hearts. It causes a rich crop to flourish within us. When we don't spend time with God, we are not focused on God and His plans, but rather on us. In order to seek the things that are above and be lifted up where we belong, we need an attitude adjustment.

Words can never adequately convey the incredible impact of our attitude toward life. The longer I live the more convinced I become that life is 10 percent what happens to us and 90 percent how we respond to it. I believe the single most significant decision I can make on a day-to-day basis is my choice of attitude. It is more important than my past, my education, my bankroll, my successes or failures, fame or pain, what other people think of me or say about me, my circumstances, or my position. Attitude keeps me going or cripples my progress. It alone fuels my fire or assaults my hope. When my attitudes are right, there's no barrier too high, no valley too deep, no dream too extreme, no challenge too great for me.[2] —*Charles Swindoll*

4. **Read Psalm 1:1-3. What do the following words mean in your life today?**

   • blessed is the [woman] who does not walk according to the world

   • [her] delight is in the law of the Lord

   • on His law [she] meditates day and night

   • [she] is like a tree . . . which yields its fruit in season

   • whatever [she] does prospers

5. **Write out Colossians 2:6-7.**

∽ What do the following words mean to you?

   • continue to live in Him

   • rooted and built up in Him

   • strengthened in the faith

   • overflowing in thanksgiving

   A few of the most wonderful by-products of understanding God's love are: peace, security, and gratitude.

When we are living with an "attitude of gratitude" in our everyday lives, we are becoming women who are living according to a new set of rules. We are setting our hearts on Christ and His purposes. We are looking for the good in all things.

> *Gratitude: the state of being grateful, thankfulness, appreciation*

Gratitude is the latest buzzword these days. Isn't it interesting how something in the Bible can be taken and applied to life and then those promoting it get all the credit for its life changing effects? The answers to all our heart's needs and longings are outlined within the practical principles of the Bible.

The Bible is full of principles to live by.

Gratitude, overflowing with thankfulness, rejoicing in all things, are just a few of the principles. These principles, however, have the ability to change our lives by changing our attitudes and the way we view things. This is a very important point.

The way you view your life affects the way you live it!

6. Write out Psalm 116:7.

7. Read Colossians 3:15-17. Rewrite each verse in your own words and personalize it. (Take note that all three verses mention thankfulness, and gratitude.)
   * verse 15

   * verse 16

   * verse 17

8. After all the instruction in chapter 3 of Colossians, Paul goes on in chapter 4 to give final instructions. Write out verse Colossians 4:2.

∽ According to Colossians 4:2, to what are you to devote yourself?

9. Again in the book of Philippians, Paul tells us to be thankful. In fact, he keeps repeating it! Write out Philippians 3:1.

∽ What do you think of that word, safeguard?

∽ Write out Philippians 4:4. (Remember that rejoice means to be joyful.)

10. Read Philippians 4:6-8. What are the key words in these verses?

∽ According to these verses, on what are you supposed to dwell?

∽ Rewrite Philippians 4:6-8 in your everyday language.

∽ Now spend some time memorizing this passage of Scripture.

11. Write out Philippians 4:9.

∽ According to this verse, what are you to put into practice?

∽ What will be the result of putting this into practice?

The Apostle Paul is a wonderful example for us to follow. We live in a world filled with heartache and disappointments . . . so did he. We live in a world where success and achievements mean putting confidence in our flesh and working hard to climb up the ladder . . . so did he. We live in a world where our minds and our hearts are locked in the prisons of disappointments and shattered dreams . . . he was in prison too. Yet in all of these things he learned to be content (Philippians 4:11) . . . and so should we.

Content: satisfied, happy, grateful

Where are you living today? Are you locked into seeing only the negative and the half-empty glass? Or are you grateful for the half-full glass that is set before you? In Philippians, Paul says that whatever we have seen him practice, we should also practice. One of the things he practiced was learning to be content. He had to learn contentment. It was not a natural trait or behavior, but rather a learned behavior.

Every woman lives in a tent: Discontent or Content

12. Write out Ephesians 4:23-24.

CO What is the key thought in these verses?

13. Read Ephesians 5:1. What do the following words say to you?
- be imitators of God

- as dearly loved children

- live a life of love

- Christ loved us and gave Himself up for us

Once we have applied our hearts to understanding God's love for us, we must then apply our hearts to learn what it means to live a life of love toward others.

Scripture tells us why we are to do that: because we are dearly loved and because Christ loved us and gave His life for us. We will be lifted to new heights as we learn to love those who do not love us, and yes even those who have actually hurt us and wronged us. By the power of the Holy Spirit, God will work His love into our lives and give us the courage to obey Him.

The first step was pouring the right foundation to build on.

Understanding God's love is the right foundation.

Now by His Spirit, He can build the house, and do His glorious work.

We each have many things to be thankful for despite our cir cumstances.

14. **Make a list of the attributes of God's love that you can now see and appreciate.**

∽ Make a list of all the people for whom you are thankful.

∽ Make a list of all the practical blessings God has given you in your everyday life.

God is stretching us, isn't He? He is stretching our values, belief systems, attitudes, and behaviors. He is stretching us in the direction of love, joy, and thankfulness. He is calling us to say no to the lies, and yes to God's truth. He does all of this for one purpose—that we might know Him and His love. And, in knowing that love, it is His plan to bring our hearts and minds to places they have never been before.

I believe God wants to change us from glory to glory, just as His Word says. He stretches us . . . extends us from one place to another . . . draws out the best in us, making us all that He has designed for us to be. Stretching can be an exciting experience—it's all in the attitude!

Stretch: to draw out to the full length; to extend from one place to another

And this is my prayer: that your love may abound more and more in knowledge and depth of insight, so that you may be able to discern what is best and may be pure and blameless until the day of Christ, filled with the fruit of righteousness that comes through Jesus Christ—to the glory and praise of God (Philippians 1:9).

Dear Lord,

May the love of God continue to lift me to higher places, places that I have never been. May Your love so fill me that I will have no need for fear or anxiety, but instead I will be able to trust in the love that never lets me go. Lord, lift me up where I belong! Amen.

THE FACTS OF PSALM 139

1. God knows me, I am not a stranger to Him.

2. He understands me as an individual.

3. He is intimately acquainted with me.

4. He knows me well enough to know what I'll say next.

5. He is covering me, I am protected.

6. He is always with me.

7. I cannot separate myself from the love of God.

8. He leads me.

9. He holds my hand.

10. My life is not in darkness, but basks in His light.

11. He made me, putting all the pieces together.

12. I am a wonderful work of God's hand.

13. My life is a miracle.

14. My days have been ordained by God.

15. His thoughts are tender toward me.

16. He is always thinking of me.

17. God preserves me from day to day.

18. When I wake to start a new day, He is still with me.

19. I am alive by His design and plan.

ENDNOTES

One: The Relationship of Love

1 Genesis 2:25

2 Genesis 3:10

3 *Roget's II, The New Thesaurus* (Boston: Houghton Mifflin Company, 1980).

4 Chuck Smith, *Why Grace Changes Everything* (Eugene, Oregon: Harvest House, 1994), p. 7.

5 Charles Stanley, *The Savior's Touch* (Grand Rapids: Zondervon, 1996), p. 67.

6 Smith, *Why Grace Changes Everything*, 1994, p. 13.

7 Hannah Whitall Smith, David Hazard, *Safe Within Your Love* (Minneapolis: Bethany House, 1992), p. 39.

8 Tim Hansel, *Keep on Dancing* (Colorado Springs: ChariotVictor Publishing, 1995), p. 119.

Two: God Is Love

1 Max Lucado, *Just Like Jesus* (Nashville: Word Books, 1998), p. 46.

2 Smith and Hazard, *Safe Within Your Love*, 1992, p. 85.

3 Oswald Chambers, *My Utmost for His Highest* (Grand Rapids: Discovery House, revised 1992), devotion for Jan. 22.

4 Andrew Murray, *The Best of Andrew Murray* (Grand Rapids: Baker Books, 1978), p. 75.

Three: Love Is Real and Practical

1 Elisabeth Elliot, *Passion and Purity* (Grand Rapids: Revell Fleming, 1984), p. 9.

2 A.W. Tozer, *Gems from Tozer* (Camp Hill, Philadelphia: Christian Publications, 1979), p. 35.

Four: Love Created Me

1 Robert McGee, *The Search for Significance* (Houston: Rapha, 1990), p. 27.

Five: Love Ordains My Days

1 Smith, *Why Grace Changes Everything*, 1994, p. 56.
2 Ruth Harms Calkin, *Lord, I Keep Running Back to You* (Wheaton: Tyndale House, Living Books, 1983), p. 11.
3 Chambers, *My Utmost for His Highest*, 1992, devotion for December 18.

Six: Love Is My Foundation

1 Title poem from *Lord, Could You Hurry a Little?* by Ruth Harms Calkins, Pomona, CA, copyright 1983. Used by permission. All rights reserved.
2 Max Lucado, *Life Lessons with Max Lucado from Hebrews: He Still Moves Stones* (Nashville: Word Publishing, 1997), p. 38.
3 Greg Laurie, *Every Day with Jesus* (Eugene, Oregon: Harvest House, 1993), p. 36.
4 Chambers, *My Utmost for His Highest*, 1992, devotion for May 7.

Seven: Love Imparts Confidence In Me

1 Barbara Johnson, *The Best of Barbara Johnson: Splashes of Joy in the Cesspool of Life* (New York: Inspirational Press, 1996), p. 301.
2 Greg Laurie, *Every Day with Jesus*, 1993, p. 15.
3 Henri J. M. Nouwen, "Prayer and the Jealous God," *New Oxford Review*, Vol. LII, June 1985, quoted on pp. 9-10 of Carol Kent's *Tame Your Fears* (Colorado Springs: NavPress, 1993).
4 McGee, *Search for Significance*, 1985, p. 8.
5 McGee, *Search for Significance*, 1985, p. 26.

Eight: Love Corrects Me

1 Billy Graham, *Unto the Hills* (as quoted in *Life Lessons with Max Lucado in Hebrews*) (Dallas: Word Publishing, 1986), p. 14.
2 Lucado, *Just Like Jesus*, 1998, p. 4.
3 Calkin, *Lord, Could You Hurry a Little?*, 1983, p. 43.
4 Lucado, *Just Like Jesus*, 1998, p. X.

Nine: Love Changes Me

1 Lucado, *Just Like Jesus*, 1998, p. X.
2 Smith, *Why Grace Changes Everything*, 1994, p. 83.
3 Smith, *Why Grace Changes Everything*, 1994, p. 86.
4 Reinhold Niebuhr, "Serenity" in Rachel Callahan and Rea McDonnell, *Adult Children of Alcoholics* (Mahwala, NJ: Paulist Press, 1990), p. 149.
5 Tozer, *Gems from Tozer*, 1979, pp. 8-9.
6 Murray, *The Best of Andrew Murray*, 1978, p. 111.
7 Laurie, *Every Day with Jesus*, 1993, p. 128.38
8 Calkin, *Lord, Could You Hurry a Little?*, 1983, p. 28

Ten: Love Gives Me Hope

1 McGee, *The Search for Significance*, 1990, pp. 29-30.
2 Lucado, *Life Lessons with Max Lucado in Hebrews*, 1997, p. 79.
3 Marie Chapian, *His Gifts to Me* (Minneapolis: Bethany House, 1988), p. 19.

Eleven: Love Has No Fear

1 Hannah Whitall Smith, *Living Confidently in God's Love* (Pittsburgh: Whittaker House, 1984), p. 37.
2 Calkin, *Lord, Could You Hurry a Little?*, 1983, p. 84.

Twelve: Love Lifts Me to New Heights

1 Will Jennings, Buffy Sainte-Marie, Jack Nitzsche, "Up Where We Belong." Copyright 1982 by Famous Music Corporation and Ensign Music Corporation, New York, NY.
2 Charles R. Swindoll, *Strengthening Your Grip* (Nashville: Word, Inc., 1982). Used by permission of *Insight for Living*, Anaheim, CA 92806.